# LAKE COMO TRAVEL GUIDE 2025

Unveiling the Secrets of Italy's Most Alluring Destination.

DARRELL KENNEDY

© **2025 by Darrell Kennedy. All rights reserved.**

No part of this book may be reproduced, distributed, or transmitted in any form or by any means, including photocopying, recording, or other electronic or mechanical methods, without the prior written permission of the author, except in the case of brief quotations embodied in critical reviews and certain other non-commercial uses permitted by copyright law.

This book is a work of non-fiction. The author has made every effort to ensure the accuracy and completeness of the information contained herein. However, the author assumes no responsibility for errors, omissions, or damages resulting from the use of the information. The author is not liable for any loss or injury caused by the use of this book. The views and opinions expressed in this book are those of the author and do not necessarily reflect the official policy or position of any organization or entity.

# TABLE OF CONTENTS.

CHAPTER 1: INTRODUCTION ................................................................ 6
    Welcome to Lake Como! ........................................................ 9
    Historical Significance. ....................................................... 10
    Why Visit Lake Como? ......................................................... 12

CHAPTER 2: GETTING THERE ............................................................. 15
    By Air: Nearest Airports and Transportation Options ..... 15
    By Train: Routes from Major Cities ................................... 19
    By Car: Driving Routes and Parking Options ................... 23

CHAPTER 3: TOP ATTRACTIONS ........................................................ 26
    Bellagio: The Pearl of Lake Como ...................................... 26
    Villa Melzi: A 19th-Century Gem ........................................ 30
    Villa del Balbianello ............................................................. 33
    Menaggio and Varenna ....................................................... 37

CHAPTER 4: ACTIVITIES .................................................................... 42
    Boat Tours: ............................................................................ 42
    Hiking .................................................................................... 47
    Cycling: Popular Routes Around the Lake ....................... 52
    Swimming: Best Spots for a Swim .................................... 56

CHAPTER 5: DINING .......................................................................... 61

Local Cuisine: Traditional Dishes to Try .......................... 61

Top Restaurants ................................................................. 65

CHAPTER 6: ACCOMMODATION ................................................. 71

Luxury Hotels................................................................... 71

Budget Options................................................................ 76

Unique Stays.................................................................... 79

CHAPTER 7: BEST TIME TO VISIT ............................................... 84

Seasonal Highlights......................................................... 84

Events and Festivals........................................................ 88

CHAPTER 8: PRACTICAL INFORMATION .................................... 93

Language: Basic Italian Phrases for Travelers ................ 93

Currency .......................................................................... 97

Safety Tips: General Safety Advice for Tourists ............ 100

CHAPTER 9: TRAVEL TIPS ........................................................ 103

Transportation: Getting Around Lake Como ................ 103

Budgeting ...................................................................... 107

Local Customs ............................................................... 111

BONUS ...................................................................................... 115

Map Guides ................................................................... 115

One Week Itinerary ....................................................... 120

CONCLUSION .......................................................................... 123

# Scan To Discover More Captivating Travel Guides for Your Next Journey.

# CHAPTER 1: INTRODUCTION

Welcome to the enchanting world of Lake Como, where breathtaking scenery, quaint villages, and timeless beauty join together to create a memorable vacation. As I write this travel guide, I am transported back to my personal journey through this Italian gem, with each memory clearly imprinted in my mind and each experience leaving an unforgettable impression on my heart.

My journey began in the bustling metropolis of Milan, a short train ride from the peaceful shores of Lake Como. As the train made its way through the undulating hills and lovely countryside, anticipation grew with each passing second.

When I got off the train in Como, I was met with the soft lapping of the lake's waters and the sight of sailboats skimming gently over its surface. "It was love at first sight."

Lake Como is a destination that offers both grandeur and intimacy, from the opulent homes that line the shore to the busy markets and cosy cafes tucked away down little lanes. I recall meandering through the cobblestone alleys of Bellagio, often known as the "Pearl of Lake Como," where each turn provided a new delight—whether it was a secret garden, a beautiful boutique, or a breathtaking view of the lake.

One of the highlights of my trip was a visit to Villa del Balbianello, an ancient villa on a wooded peninsula. Its breathtaking gardens and panoramic views of the lake are the stuff of dreams, and as I walked through its hallowed corridors, I couldn't help but feel a strong connection to the history and stories that have unfolded within its walls.

Lake Como is more than simply its beautiful splendour; it is a treasure mine of experiences ready to be explored.

This region has something for everyone, whether they want to go on a leisurely boat excursion, hike the trails of the surrounding Alps, or savour the rich flavours of Lombard cuisine in a lakeside trattoria. Every moment, whether spent in the lively town of Menaggio or the tranquil village of Varenna, is an opportunity to make memories that will last a lifetime.

This travel guide was created out of my real passion for Lake Como and a desire to share its wonders with other travellers.

This guide, which includes thorough information on attractions, activities, restaurants, and practical recommendations, intends to be your reliable companion as you embark on your own Lake Como adventure. Pack your bags, bring your sense of wonder, and prepare to visit one of the world's most enchanting destinations. Welcome to Lake Como!

# **<u>Welcome to Lake Como!</u>**

Imagine a place where the sky meets sapphire-blue waters, where beautiful mountainsides cradle attractive communities, and elegant villas peek through the forest. This is Lake Como, a place that seamlessly combines natural beauty, historical significance, and engaging culture.

When I first saw the lake, I was struck by its tranquilly. The smooth lapping of water against ancient stone, the aroma of flowering wisteria, and the sight of colourful buildings clinging to the hillsides all combined to create a sensory symphony. It's no surprise that Lake Como has enchanted painters, writers, and tourists for generations.

This picturesque refuge has been a hideaway for celebrities such as Alessandro Volta, the physicist who invented the electric battery, and, more recently, Hollywood star George Clooney, who has a property in Laglio. Their presence reveals much about the lake's lasting appeal.

Lake Como has something for everyone, whether you want to go hiking in the neighbouring Alps, relax in a lakeside garden, or immerse yourself in history. This guide will be your key to discovering the enchantment of this unique place.

## Historical Significance.

Lake Como's landscape tells a wonderful story that spans millennia. From its prehistoric origins to its present attraction, the lake has seen empires rise and fall, art and commerce grow, and the eternal spirit of Italian life.

Evidence suggests that the lake's beaches have been populated since the Bronze Age. Later, the Romans saw its strategic value and founded the city of Como in 196 BC. They were drawn to its fertile grounds and strategic location, developing it into a thriving commercial and agricultural centre.

During the Middle Ages, Como evolved as a silk powerhouse, with talented artisans manufacturing exquisite materials for Europe's elite.

This affluence fuelled the development of magnificent churches and palazzos, which influenced the city's architectural style.

The Renaissance ushered forth a new era of change, as wealthy families constructed luxurious mansions along the lake's shores. These architectural marvels, with their beautiful gardens and panoramic views, were symbols of power and luxury. Many of these mansions, such as Villa Carlotta and Villa del Balbianello, are now open to visitors, providing insights into a bygone era of luxury.

Lake Como flourished in the nineteenth century as a sanctuary for artists and intellectuals looking for inspiration and solace. Composers like Franz Liszt and Gioachino Rossini found consolation in its tranquil beauty, while poets like Stendhal and Mary Shelley were inspired by its dramatic scenery.

Lake Como continues to attract people from throughout the world. Its timeless beauty, rich history, and dynamic culture make it the ultimate destination.

## Why Visit Lake Como?

Beyond the picture-perfect postcards and Instagram-worthy panoramas, Lake Como has a plethora of experiences to satisfy every traveler's needs. Whether you want adventure, leisure, cultural immersion, or a taste of the high life, you can find it here.

**Embrace the Active Lifestyle:**

- Boating: Use a boat to explore the lake's hidden coves, lovely villages, and majestic villas. Rent a kayak or paddleboard for a more intimate encounter, take a public ferry for a picturesque trip, or book a private boat cruise for a sumptuous journey.

- Hiking: Lace up your boots and explore the magnificent trails that wind across the neighbouring Alps. There's a walk for every fitness level and desire, from easy lakeside trails to strenuous mountain climbs.
- Cycling: Follow the picturesque roads that skirt the lake's shores, enjoying panoramic views and quaint communities along the way. For a more difficult ride, explore the mountain trails and feel the rush of downhill riding.
- Swimming: Enjoy a relaxing plunge in the lake's crystal-clear waters. Choose between public beaches, exclusive lidos with amenities, and hidden coves for a more intimate experience.

**Immerse yourself with culture and history.**

- Villa Visits: Travel back in time and discover the beautiful villas that line the lakefront. Wander through groomed gardens, view gorgeous buildings, and learn about the families that formerly lived on these grand estates.
- Historic towns: Discover the picturesque cities and villages that surround the lake, each with its own distinct character and history. Wander through cobblestone alleyways, admire antique churches and palazzos, and experience the true Italian atmosphere.
- Museums and Art: Explore the region's rich cultural legacy via its museums and art galleries. Discover the works of local painters, the history of silk manufacture, and Alessandro Volta's scientific accomplishments.

**Indulge in the finer things.**

- Gastronomy: Experience the flavours of Lake Como's food scene. Enjoy fresh lake fish, creamy risotto, substantial polenta meals, and local cheeses. Pair your dinner with a glass of local wine to celebrate the Italian tradition of unhurried cuisine and good company.
- Luxury Accommodation: Spend your vacation in a beautiful lakeside hotel or villa. Enjoy outstanding service, stunning views, and first-rate amenities. Relax by the pool, enjoy spa treatments, and savour exquisite dinners with magnificent views.

**Find the perfect pace:**

- Relaxation: Get away from the stress and bustle of everyday life and unwind in the peaceful surroundings of Lake Como. Find a quiet area by the lake, read a book in a gorgeous garden, or simply enjoy the peacefulness of your surroundings.
- Romance: Lake Como is a great place for a romantic getaway because it has beautiful scenery, cute towns, and high-end accommodations. Stroll hand in hand along the shoreline, have a candlelit meal with lake views, or escape to a quiet villa for an intimate getaway.

Lake Como provides an exceptional experience for all travellers, whether they desire adventure, relaxation, or a taste of the Italian dolce vita.

# CHAPTER 2: GETTING THERE

## By Air: Nearest Airports and Transportation Options

Lake Como is easily accessible from three main airports in the Lombardy region.

- Milan Malpensa Airport (MXP) is the major international airport in the area, located around 50 kilometres (31 miles) from Como.
- Milan Linate Airport (LIN): A minor airport near Milan's city centre, around 80 kilometres (50 miles) from Como.
- Bergamo Orio al Serio Airport (BGY): This airport, which predominantly serves low-cost aircraft, is around 95 kilometres (59 miles) from Como.

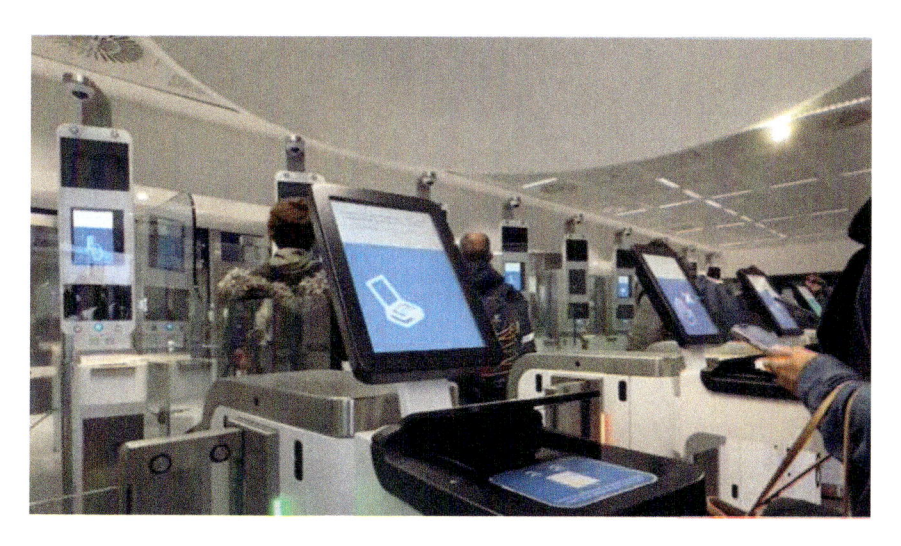

## Transportation Options for Each Airport:

### Milan Malpensa (MXP):

- Train: The Malpensa Express provides a direct connection to Como San Giovanni train station (about one hour). Trains leave routinely from Terminal 1.

- Bus: Several bus companies provide services from Malpensa to Como town centre (about 1 hour and 15 minutes).
- Taxi: Taxis are widely available outside the airport terminal. Expect a one-hour journey with a price of around €100-€130.
- Private Transfer: Pre-booked private transports are a convenient and comfortable option, with door-to-door service and fixed fares.

## Milan Linate (LIN):

- Bus: Take a bus from Linate to Milan Central Station, then transfer to a train to Como San Giovanni (travel duration roughly 2 hours).
- Taxi: Taxis are accessible outside the airport terminal, with a travel duration of about 1 hour 30 minutes and a price of around €150-€200.
- Pre-booked private shuttles provide a flawless ride to your Lake Como destination.

## Bergamo Orio Al Serio (BGY):

- Bus: Direct bus service runs from Bergamo Airport to Como town centre (about 1 hour 30 minutes).

- Train: Take a bus from the airport to Bergamo train station, then transfer to a train to Como San Giovanni (travel duration roughly 2 hours).
- Taxis are accessible outside the airport terminal, however the trip to Lake Como might be costly (about €180-€250).
- Pre-booked private transfers are a good choice for a comfortable and hassle-free ride.

### Tips for Scheduling Transportation in Advance:

- Train tickets: Buy train tickets online in advance, especially during high season, to get the best deals and avoid long lines at the station.
- Bus tickets: View bus schedules and purchase tickets online or at the airport bus terminal.
- Private transfers: Several companies provide private transfer services. Compare costs and book ahead of time to assure availability and the sort of vehicle you want.

### Information on Private Transfer Services:

- Private transfers offer a more personalised and comfortable mode of transportation, particularly for families or parties travelling with luggage.
- Drivers often greet you in the airport arrival area with a name sign and assist you with your luggage.
- Vehicles range from standard automobiles to luxury sedans and minivans, depending on your requirements and budget.

- Pre-booking a private transfer guarantees a fixed fee and eliminates the inconvenience of navigating public transport or hailing a cab.

**Private Transfer Service:**

- Shuttle Direct: Offers a range of transfer options from all three airports to Lake Como.
- Welcome Pickups: Provides meet-and-greet services with English-speaking drivers

By carefully evaluating your budget, travel style, and arrival airport, you may select the best mode of transportation for your trip to Lake Como.

## By Train: Routes from Major Cities

Travelling to Lake Como by rail is a picturesque and convenient choice, especially if you're coming from another large Italian city. The primary train station serving Lake Como is Como San Giovanni, which is located in the middle of Como.

**Major Train Routes with Connecting Stations:**

- From Milan, trains depart frequently from Milano Centrale, Milano Porta Garibaldi, and Milano Cadorna to Como San Giovanni. The trek takes about 30 to 50 minutes.

- From Rome: Take the high-speed rail from Roma Termini to Milano Centrale, then transfer to a regional train to Como San Giovanni.
- From Florence: Travel from Firenze Santa Maria Novella to Milano Centrale, then transfer to a regional train to Como San Giovanni (total journey time approximately 3-4 hours).
- From Venice: Take the high-speed rail from Venezia Santa Lucia to Milano Centrale, then transfer to a regional train to Como San Giovanni.

**Train operators:**

- Trenitalia: The national train operator in Italy, offering a wide range of train types and services.
- Italo: A private high-speed train operator that provides services on significant lines, including connections to Milan.

## Types Of Trains And Travel Times:

- High-speed trains (Frecciarossa, Frecciargento, Italo) provide quick and pleasant connections between major cities. Travel time from Rome, Florence, and Venice to Milan ranges between 2 and 3 hours.
- Regional trains (Regionale, Regionale Veloce) connect smaller towns and cities, and provide frequent service to Como San Giovanni from Milan and the neighbouring areas. Travel time from Milan to Como ranges between 30 and 50 minutes.

## Information on Purchasing Train Tickets:

- Online: You can buy rail tickets from Trenitalia (www.trenitalia.com) or Italo (www.italotreno.it). Online booking allows you to compare rates, select your preferred seats, and avoid lines at the station.

- Train tickets can be purchased at ticket counters and self-service devices in major train stations.

**Tips for navigating the Italian train system:**

- Validate your ticket: Before you board any train in Italy, make sure to validate your ticket at one of the yellow validation devices available on the platforms.
- Check the platform information: Pay attention to platform announcements and display boards, since platform numbers may change.
- Be aware of the train types: Different train types offer varying degrees of comfort and speed. Consider your budget and travel time while selecting a train.
- Store your bags securely: Keep your luggage close to you on the train and be cautious of your things in crowded stops.
- Learn basic Italian phrases: Knowing a few basic Italian phrases will help you interact with train workers or ask for directions.

You can enjoy a smooth and efficient travel to Lake Como if you plan your rail journey ahead of time and are familiar with the Italian train system.

# By Car: Driving Routes and Parking Options

**Driving Routes to Lake Como**

- From Milan, the most direct route is via the A9/E35 motorway, which takes around an hour and ten minutes. Alternatively, you can take the picturesque SS340, which takes approximately 1 hour and 30 minutes and provides stunning views of the lake.
- From Venice, use the A4/E64 route, which takes approximately 3.5 to 4 hours. Consider taking the SS36 and SS38 for a more scenic drive that will add an hour to your trip but provide stunning views.

- From Florence, the fastest route is the A1/E35 highway, which takes about 4 to 5 hours. For a more leisurely trip, choose the SS62 and SS38, which take around 6 hours but provide beautiful landscape.

- From Rome, the A1/E35 highway is the quickest option, lasting approximately 7 to 8 hours. For a more picturesque journey, choose the SS2 and SS38, which will take around 9 hours but provide breathtaking scenery.

## Estimated Driving Time and Distance

- Milan to Lake Como takes around an hour and ten minutes (50 km).
- Venice to Lake Como takes about 3.5 to 4 hours (250 kilometres).
- Florence to Lake Como takes about 4 to 5 hours (300 kilometres).
- Rome to Lake Como takes about 7 to 8 hours (500 kilometres).

## Tips for navigating the roads around Lake Como.

- Plan Ahead: To prevent congestion, check traffic conditions and plan your route ahead of time.
- Drive safely: Use caution on narrow roads and keep an eye out for pedestrians and cyclists.
- Enjoy the Scenery: Take breaks to admire the magnificent scenery and explore the quaint communities along the road.

## Information about Tolls and Vignettes

- Tolls: Some roadways, including the A9/E35, may charge tolls. Check the official website for toll pricing and payment alternatives.

- Vignettes are not required while driving around Lake Como.

**Parking options and associated costs**

- Autosilo Centro Lago's address is Via S. Elia 6, Como. Fees: €0.50 every half-hour, €2.50 for the first hour, and €2.50 for each additional hour.
- Autosilo Comunale: Address: Via Auguadri 1, Como. Fees: 6:30 AM to 20:30: €1.00 for the first and second hours, €1.55 for each subsequent hour.
- Autosilo Jasca's address is Piazza Volta 42, Como. Fees: €3.00 per hour during the day; €1.50 for the first half-hour.
- Autosilo 4° Ponte's address is Viale Innocenzo XI 77, Como. Fees: €2.00 per hour from 8:00 a.m. to 20:00 p.m., €1.00 per hour after that.
- Autosilo Università's address is Via Castelnuovo, Como. Fees: €0.50 for the first half-hour, followed by €2.50 for each additional hour from 7:00 AM to 13:00.

**ZTL (Limited Traffic Zone) Information**

- Como: The city centre is a ZTL, with access limited to authorised cars only. Check for signage and adhere to local restrictions.
- Bellagio: The historic centre becomes a pedestrian zone from 9:40 a.m. to 5:00 a.m. the next day. A monitoring system controls access.

# CHAPTER 3: TOP ATTRACTIONS

## Bellagio: The Pearl of Lake Como

Nestled at the tip of the peninsula where Lake Como's three branches converge, Bellagio truly lives up to its moniker, "The Pearl of Lake Como." This picturesque village captivates visitors with its elegant villas, colorful gardens, vibrant atmosphere, and stunning views.

### Historical Background:

Bellagio's history dates back to Roman times, but it truly flourished during the Renaissance and became a popular destination for the European aristocracy in the 18th and 19th centuries. This rich past is reflected in its grand villas, charming streets, and historic landmarks.

**Key Landmarks:**

- **Punta Spartivento:** This iconic point offers panoramic views of all three branches of the lake. It's the perfect spot for capturing breathtaking photos and soaking in the beauty of the surrounding landscape.

- **Basilica di San Giacomo:** This Romanesque church, dating back to the 12th century, boasts beautiful frescoes and a peaceful atmosphere.

- **Grand Hotel Villa Serbelloni:** This historic luxury hotel, once a private villa, is known for its opulent interiors, stunning gardens, and breathtaking views.

**Shopping Streets and Local Crafts:**

- **Via Garibaldi:** This charming pedestrian street is lined with boutiques, shops, and cafes. You'll find a variety of souvenirs, local crafts, and high-end fashion.

- **Salita Serbelloni:** This scenic staircase leads up to Villa Serbelloni and offers stunning views of the lake. Along the way, you'll find charming shops and art galleries.

- **Local Crafts:** Bellagio is known for its silk production, and you can find beautiful silk scarves, ties, and other items in local shops.

**Dining Scene Overview:**

- Bellagio offers a diverse culinary scene, with options to suit every taste and budget.

- **Fine dining:** Enjoy gourmet cuisine with breathtaking lake views at restaurants like Mistral at Grand Hotel Villa Serbelloni or La Terrazza at Hotel Splendide Royal.

- **Traditional trattorias:** Savor authentic Italian dishes and local specialties at charming trattorias like Trattoria San Giacomo or La Grotta.

- **Cafes and bars:** Relax with a coffee or aperitivo at one of Bellagio's many cafes and bars, many with outdoor seating overlooking the lake.

**Walking Tours and Day Trip Suggestions:**

- **Walking tours:** Explore Bellagio's historic center and charming streets on a guided walking tour. Learn about the village's history, architecture, and culture.

- **Boat trips:** Take a boat trip to other picturesque villages around the lake, such as Varenna, Menaggio, or Tremezzo.

- **Villa Melzi Gardens:** Explore the beautiful gardens of Villa Melzi, featuring a variety of plants, sculptures, and stunning lake views.

- **Villa del Balbianello:** Visit this historic villa with its terraced gardens and panoramic views, featured in several movies.

With its captivating beauty, rich history, and abundance of attractions, Bellagio is a must-visit destination on any Lake Como itinerary.

# Villa Melzi: A 19th-Century Gem

Overlooking the shimmering waters of Lake Como, Villa Melzi stands as a testament to the elegance and grandeur of the early 19th century. This neoclassical masterpiece, with its meticulously landscaped gardens, offers visitors a glimpse into a bygone era of aristocratic splendor.

### History of the Villa and its Owners:

Built between 1808 and 1810, Villa Melzi was commissioned by Francesco Melzi d'Eril, Duke of Lodi and vice-president of the Italian Republic under Napoleon. Melzi, a close friend and confidant of Napoleon, envisioned a serene retreat where he could entertain dignitaries and enjoy the beauty of Lake Como.

After Melzi's death, the villa passed to his descendants, the Gallarati Scotti family, who continue to own and maintain this historical treasure.

**Architectural Features and Design:**

Designed by the renowned architect Giocondo Albertolli, Villa Melzi embodies the principles of neoclassical architecture. Its symmetrical façade, adorned with Ionic columns and elegant statues, exudes a sense of harmony and balance. The villa's interior, although not open to the public, is said to be equally impressive, featuring ornate decorations and period furnishings.

The villa's expansive gardens, spanning over 8 hectares (20 acres), are a masterpiece of landscape design. Created by Luigi Canonica and Alessandro Manzoni, the gardens seamlessly blend formal elements with the natural beauty of the lakeshore.

**Key highlights of the gardens include:**

- **The Water Garden:** This serene oasis features a picturesque pond with water lilies, surrounded by lush vegetation and sculptures.

- **The English-style Park:** This expansive parkland features winding paths, towering trees, and a collection of exotic plants from around the world.

- **The Chapel:** A small, neoclassical chapel dedicated to St. Francis, adorned with frescoes and sculptures.

- **The Orangery:** A beautiful glasshouse used to shelter citrus trees during the winter months, now housing a museum with archaeological artifacts and sculptures.

- **The Museum:** Located within the Orangery, the museum showcases a collection of Roman and Etruscan artifacts, as well as sculptures and memorabilia related to the Melzi family.

**Opening Hours, Entrance Fees, and Guided Tour Information:**

- **Opening Hours:** The gardens are generally open from late March to late October, daily from 9:30 AM to 6:30 PM.

- **Entrance Fees:** As of December 2024, the entrance fee is €8.00 for adults. Reduced prices are available for children, groups, and seniors.

- **Guided Tours:** Guided tours of the gardens are available, offering insights into the history, design, and botanical significance of the estate. Check the official website or inquire at the ticket office for tour schedules and availability.

**Website:** www.villamelzi.it

A visit to Villa Melzi is a journey through time and beauty. Its elegant architecture, meticulously curated gardens, and serene atmosphere offer a truly unforgettable experience on Lake Como.

## Villa del Balbianello

Perched on the tip of the wooded Lavedo peninsula, Villa del Balbianello is a masterpiece of Italian architecture and garden design. Its breathtaking views, elegant interiors, and fascinating history make it one of Lake Como's most captivating attractions.

**Historical Background and Past Owners:**

Originally the site of a Franciscan monastery, Villa del Balbianello was transformed into a luxurious private residence in the late 18th century by Cardinal Angelo Maria Durini. He envisioned a place of tranquility and intellectual pursuit, where he could escape the bustle of city life and enjoy the beauty of the lake.

After Durini's death, the villa passed through several owners, each leaving their mark on its history and design. In the 19th century, it was acquired by Count Luigi Porro Lambertenghi, who added the loggia and enhanced the gardens.

The villa's most recent owner, the explorer and businessman Guido Monzino, left a lasting legacy. He filled the villa with his collection of art, artifacts, and memorabilia from his expeditions around the world, creating a unique and eclectic atmosphere. Upon his death in 1988, Monzino bequeathed the villa to the Fondo Ambiente Italiano (FAI), ensuring its preservation for future generations.

**Architectural Highlights and Interior Design:**

Villa del Balbianello's architecture is a blend of styles, reflecting its layered history. The main building features a distinctive loggia with twisted columns, offering panoramic views of the lake. Inside, visitors can explore exquisitely decorated rooms filled with Monzino's collection of antique furniture, paintings, and maps. The library, with its intricate wood paneling and collection of rare books, is a particular highlight.

**Gardens and Panoramic Views:**

The villa's terraced gardens are a masterpiece of landscaping, cascading down to the lake's edge. Manicured hedges, colorful flowerbeds, and ancient trees create a serene and picturesque setting.

From the gardens, visitors can enjoy breathtaking views of Lake Como, including the picturesque village of Lenno, the Isola Comacina (the only island on the lake), and the surrounding mountains. The panoramic vista from the villa's loggia is particularly spectacular, offering a 270-degree view of the lake's western branch.

**Information on Accessing the Villa:**

- **By Boat:** The most common way to reach Villa del Balbianello is by boat. Regular ferry services operate from Lenno and other lakeside towns. Private boat tours and water taxis are also available.

- **Walking Path:** A scenic walking path leads from Lenno to the villa, offering a pleasant stroll through the woods (approximately 20-30 minutes).

**Opening Hours, Entrance Fees, and Guided Tour Options:**

- **Opening Hours:** The villa and gardens are generally open from mid-March to early November, with specific days and times varying depending on the season. It's advisable to check the official website for the most up-to-date information.

- **Entrance Fees:** As of December 2024, the entrance fee is €20.00 for adults. Reduced prices are available for children, students, and FAI members.

- **Guided Tours:** Guided tours are available in Italian and English, offering insights into the villa's history, architecture, and collections. Tours must be booked in advance through the FAI website.

**Website:** www.fondoambiente.it/luoghi/villa-del-balbianello

A visit to Villa del Balbianello is a truly unforgettable experience. Its stunning location, elegant architecture, and fascinating history make it a must-see destination on any Lake Como itinerary.

## Menaggio and Varenna

Often referred to as the "Golden Triangle," the central area of Lake Como boasts some of its most captivating villages. Menaggio and Varenna, situated on opposite shores, offer distinct charms and experiences, making them essential stops on any Lake Como adventure.

**Menaggio:**

This vibrant resort town exudes a lively and welcoming atmosphere, making it an ideal destination for families and those seeking a more active holiday.

- **Family-Friendly Appeal:** Menaggio offers a range of activities suitable for all ages, from leisurely strolls along the lakefront to exciting water sports and boat excursions. The town's relaxed ambiance and ample amenities cater to families with children.

- **Waterfront Promenade:** Menaggio's picturesque promenade stretches along the lake, offering stunning views and a perfect setting for leisurely walks, cycling, or simply enjoying an ice cream while soaking up the atmosphere.

- **Lido di Menaggio:** This popular lido provides a designated area for swimming and sunbathing, with facilities including changing rooms, showers, and a bar. It's a great place to cool off on a hot summer day.

- **Excursions:** Menaggio serves as an excellent base for exploring other attractions around the lake. Ferries depart regularly to Bellagio, Varenna, and other picturesque villages. You can also easily access Villa Carlotta and Villa del Balbianello from here.

**Varenna:**

With its pastel-colored houses cascading down the hillside to the water's edge, Varenna exudes a romantic and tranquil charm.

- **Charming Atmosphere:** Varenna's relaxed pace and picturesque setting create an idyllic escape from the hustle and bustle of everyday life. Its narrow cobblestone streets, waterfront cafes, and colorful houses invite leisurely exploration.

- **Villa Monastero:** This historic villa, once a Cistercian monastery, now houses a museum with botanical gardens and stunning lake views. Explore the villa's elegant interiors and wander through the terraced gardens adorned with exotic plants and sculptures.

- **Castello di Vezio:** Perched on a hill overlooking Varenna, this medieval castle offers panoramic views of the lake and surrounding landscape. Explore the castle's towers, ramparts, and gardens, and learn about its fascinating history.

- **Hiking Trails and Scenic Viewpoints:** Varenna is a haven for outdoor enthusiasts. Numerous hiking trails lead from the village into the surrounding hills, offering breathtaking views of the lake and mountains. The Sentiero del Viandante, an ancient pathway that winds along the eastern shore, is a particularly popular option.

**Key Differences:**

While both Menaggio and Varenna offer captivating beauty and unique experiences, they cater to slightly different preferences:

- **Atmosphere:** Menaggio is more lively and bustling, while Varenna is more tranquil and relaxed.

- **Activities:** Menaggio offers more family-friendly activities and water sports, while Varenna is better suited for those seeking hiking and exploring historic sites.

- **Accommodation:** Menaggio has a wider range of hotels and resorts, while Varenna offers more intimate and charming accommodation options.

Whether you choose to soak up the vibrant atmosphere of Menaggio or embrace the tranquil charm of Varenna, both villages offer an unforgettable experience in the heart of Lake Como's Golden Triangle.

# CHAPTER 4: ACTIVITIES

## Boat Tours:

Experiencing Lake Como from the water is an absolute must. The shimmering expanse of the lake, framed by majestic mountains and dotted with picturesque villages, reveals its true splendor from a boat's perspective.

Whether you crave the freedom of independent exploration or the insights of a guided tour, there's a boating experience tailored to your desires.

## Public Ferries:

Navigazione Laghi, the public ferry service, offers a comprehensive network connecting the towns and villages that dot the lake's shores. It's an affordable and efficient way to travel, providing a taste of local life and stunning views along the way.

- **Routes and Timetables:** Ferries crisscross the lake, linking major hubs like Como, Bellagio, Varenna, Menaggio, and Tremezzo, as well as smaller villages. Detailed timetables, which vary by season and route, are available on the Navigazione Laghi website (www.navigazionelaghi.it) and their user-friendly app.

**Types of Ferries:**

- **Traghetti (Slow Ferries):** These traditional ferries offer a leisurely pace, perfect for soaking in the scenery and capturing photos.

- **Aliscafi (Fast Ferries):** Hydrofoils that zip across the lake, ideal for those prioritizing speed and efficiency.

- **Car Ferries:** Transport vehicles across the lake, primarily between Varenna and Bellagio/Menaggio.

**Tickets and Fares:** Tickets can be purchased at ferry terminals, on board (sometimes with a surcharge), or online. Fares are calculated based on distance and ferry type. Consider purchasing a day pass for unlimited travel if you plan on hopping between multiple villages.

**Private Boat Rental:**

For those seeking autonomy and a personalized experience, renting a private boat unlocks the lake's hidden coves and allows for customized itineraries.

- **Options and Costs:** A diverse fleet awaits, from nimble motorboats ideal for couples to spacious powerboats perfect for families, and even luxurious yachts for those seeking ultimate indulgence. Rental costs fluctuate depending on the boat's size, type, duration of rental, and season. Expect to pay from €80 per hour for a small motorboat to upwards of €1,000 per day for a luxury yacht.

- **License Requirements:** In Italy, boats with engines exceeding 40 horsepower generally require a boating license. However, smaller boats, often those rented to tourists, may not. Always confirm license requirements with the rental company before booking.

- **Fuel Costs:** Fuel is typically not included in the rental price. Be sure to factor in fuel consumption, as it can add a significant amount to the overall cost, especially for longer journeys or powerful engines.

## Water Taxis:

Water taxis provide a luxurious and efficient way to travel directly to your destination, bypassing ferry schedules and offering personalized service.

- **Services and Fares:** Water taxis can be hailed at designated points along the lake or pre-booked through various companies. Fares are calculated based on distance, time, and the number of passengers. Expect to pay a premium for this convenient service.

- **Advantages:** Ideal for reaching villas or hotels with private docks, transferring between towns quickly, or enjoying a romantic sunset cruise.

## Guided Boat Tours and Themed Cruises:

For a deeper understanding of the lake's history, culture, and hidden gems, guided boat tours offer a curated experience.

**Types of Tours:**

- **Sightseeing Tours:** Explore iconic landmarks, charming villages, and historic villas with commentary from knowledgeable guides.

- **Sunset Cruises:** Enjoy the magic of a Lake Como sunset with a glass of prosecco in hand.

- **Wine Tasting Tours:** Combine a scenic boat trip with visits to local vineyards for tastings of regional wines.

- **Private Villa Tours:** Gain exclusive access to private villas and gardens not typically open to the public.

- **Photography Tours:** Capture the lake's beauty with guidance from professional photographers.

**Benefits:** Guided tours provide historical context, local insights, and access to exclusive locations, enriching your overall experience.

## Tips for Choosing the Right Boat Tour:

- **Budget:** Public ferries are the most budget-friendly, while private rentals and water taxis cater to higher budgets.

- **Itinerary:** Align your boat choice with your desired destinations and travel style.

- **Preferences:** Consider your preference for speed, flexibility, and guided experiences.
- **Group Size:** Choose a boat that comfortably accommodates your group.
- **Advance Bookings:** Secure your preferred boat tour or rental by booking in advance, especially during peak season.

## Hiking

Lake Como's beauty isn't confined to its shimmering waters. The surrounding Alps rise majestically, offering a network of hiking trails that cater to all levels, from leisurely strolls to challenging climbs. Lace up your boots, breathe in the fresh mountain air, and discover hidden waterfalls, panoramic vistas, and charming villages nestled amidst the peaks.

**Greenway del Lago di Como:**

This relatively new path, completed in 2018, offers a gentle and accessible introduction to the lake's natural beauty.

- **Difficulty:** Easy
- **Length:** 10 km (6.2 miles)
- **Elevation Gain:** Minimal
- **Route:** The Greenway winds along the western shore of the lake, connecting the villages of Colonno, Sala Comacina, Ossuccio, Lenno, Mezzegra, Tremezzo, and Griante.
- **Highlights:** Stroll through charming villages, admire historic villas, and enjoy breathtaking lake views. The path is mostly flat and paved, making it suitable for families with strollers and people with limited mobility.
- **Access Points:** Access the Greenway from any of the villages it connects.

**Sentiero del Viandante:**

This historic trail, once a vital trade route, offers a journey through time and breathtaking scenery.

- **Difficulty:** Moderate
- **Length:** 45 km (28 miles)
- **Elevation Gain:** Significant, with some steep sections
- **Route:** The Sentiero del Viandante follows the eastern shore of the lake, from Abbadia Lariana in the north to

Colico in the south. It's typically divided into four stages, each offering unique landscapes and charming villages.

- **Highlights:** Hike through ancient forests, pass by historic churches and castles, and enjoy panoramic views of the lake and surrounding mountains.

- **Access Points:** Access the trail from various points along the eastern shore, including Abbadia Lariana, Mandello del Lario, Varenna, and Bellano.

**Monte San Primo:**

For experienced hikers seeking a challenge and rewarding views, Monte San Primo offers a summit experience.

- **Difficulty:** Challenging
- **Length:** Various trails, ranging from 7 km (4.3 miles) to 15 km (9.3 miles)

- **Elevation Gain:** Significant, reaching 1,682 meters (5,518 feet) at the summit.
- **Route:** Several trails ascend Monte San Primo, starting from different points around the mountain.
- **Highlights:** Conquer challenging terrain, pass through diverse landscapes, and enjoy panoramic views of Lake Como, the surrounding valleys, and the Alps. On clear days, you can even see the distant city of Milan.
- **Access Points:** Access trails from Bellagio, Nesso, and other villages around the mountain.

### Other Hiking Trails:

Numerous other trails cater to diverse interests and abilities.

- **Sentiero delle Espressioni:** This artistic trail near Varenna features contemporary sculptures integrated into the natural landscape.
- **Monte Grona:** A challenging hike with rewarding views of the lake's central basin.
- **Val di Mello:** A valley known for its dramatic granite cliffs and waterfalls, offering various hiking options.

**Tips for Hiking Safety and Preparation:**

- **Plan your route:** Choose a trail that matches your fitness level and experience.

- **Check weather conditions:** Mountain weather can be unpredictable, so check the forecast before you go.

- **Wear appropriate footwear:** Wear sturdy hiking boots with good ankle support.

- **Pack essentials:** Bring water, snacks, sunscreen, a hat, a map, and a first-aid kit.

- **Inform someone of your plans:** Let someone know your hiking route and expected return time.

- **Stay on marked trails:** Avoid venturing off marked trails to minimize the risk of getting lost.

- **Be aware of wildlife:** Be cautious of wildlife, especially snakes and wild boars.

- **Respect the environment:** Pack out all trash and avoid disturbing the natural environment.

# Cycling: Popular Routes Around the Lake

Lake Como's scenic beauty and diverse terrain make it a paradise for cyclists. Whether you prefer leisurely rides along the waterfront, challenging climbs through mountain passes, or exhilarating descents on off-road trails, there's a route to suit your skill level and interests.

**Lakeside Cycling Paths:**

For a relaxed and scenic ride, several dedicated cycling paths offer gentle terrain and breathtaking views.

- **Greenway del Lago di Como:** This 10 km (6.2 mile) path, mostly flat and paved, winds along the western shore of the lake, connecting picturesque villages and offering stunning lake vistas. It's perfect for families and those seeking a leisurely pace.

- **Ciclovia dei Laghi:** This longer route, stretching for over 100 km (62 miles), connects several lakes in the region, including Lake Como, Lake Lugano, and Lake Varese. The Lake Como section offers a mix of lakeside paths and quiet roads, suitable for moderate cyclists.

**Road Cycling Routes:**

For those seeking a more challenging ride, numerous road cycling routes offer varying levels of difficulty and breathtaking scenery.

- **Western Shore Route:** This route, following the SS340 Regina state road, offers a scenic ride along the western shore of the lake. It features some gentle climbs and descents, making it suitable for intermediate cyclists.

- **Ghisallo Climb:** A legendary climb for cycling enthusiasts, the Ghisallo ascent is known for its challenging gradients and stunning views. It's a must-do for experienced riders.

- **Madonna del Ghisallo:** Located at the top of the Ghisallo climb, this sanctuary dedicated to the patron saint of cyclists is a popular pilgrimage site for cycling enthusiasts.

- **Muro di Sormano:** For a truly challenging climb, the Muro di Sormano is a short but incredibly steep ascent with gradients reaching over 25%. It's a test for even the most seasoned cyclists.

**Mountain Biking Trails:**

The mountains surrounding Lake Como offer a network of thrilling mountain biking trails, catering to different skill levels.

- **Val di Mello:** This valley, known for its dramatic granite cliffs and waterfalls, offers a variety of challenging mountain biking trails.

- **Monte San Primo:** The trails around Monte San Primo offer a mix of uphill climbs and exhilarating descents, with stunning views of the lake and surrounding mountains.

- **Sentiero del Viandante:** While primarily a hiking trail, some sections of the Sentiero del Viandante are suitable for mountain biking, offering a unique perspective on the lake's eastern shore.

## Information on Bike Rental Shops and Guided Cycling Tours:

- **Bike Rental Shops:** Numerous bike rental shops are located around the lake, offering a variety of bikes, including road bikes, mountain bikes, e-bikes, and city bikes. Some shops also offer accessories like helmets, locks, and maps.

- **Guided Cycling Tours:** Several companies offer guided cycling tours, catering to different interests and skill levels. These tours provide a safe and informative way to explore the region, with experienced guides leading the way and sharing insights into the local history and culture.

## Tips for Cycling Around Lake Como:

- **Choose the right bike:** Select a bike that suits your riding style and the terrain you plan to tackle.

- **Plan your route:** Research cycling routes in advance and choose one that matches your fitness level and interests.

- **Check weather conditions:** Be aware of weather conditions, especially wind and rain, which can affect your ride.

- **Wear appropriate gear:** Wear comfortable cycling clothing, including a helmet, gloves, and sunglasses.

- **Bring essentials:** Pack water, snacks, sunscreen, a repair kit, and a map.

- **Be aware of traffic:** Share the road with other vehicles and be mindful of pedestrians.

- **Respect the environment:** Stay on designated trails and avoid littering.

## Swimming: Best Spots for a Swim

Lake Como's crystal-clear waters beckon on a hot summer day. Whether you prefer the amenities of a lido or the tranquility of a secluded cove, there are numerous spots to enjoy a refreshing dip and soak up the sun.

**Public Beaches:**

- **Lido di Menaggio:** This popular public beach offers a spacious area for swimming and sunbathing. Facilities include changing rooms, showers, restrooms, a bar, and a restaurant. Sun loungers and umbrellas are available for rent.

- **Lido di Argegno:** Located in the charming village of Argegno, this lido offers a sandy beach, a swimming pool, and a playground, making it a great option for families.

- **Lido di Lenno:** Situated near Villa del Balbianello, this lido provides stunning views and a relaxed atmosphere.

- **Other Public Beaches:** Several smaller public beaches are scattered around the lake, often accessible via walking paths or by boat. Look for signs indicating "spiaggia libera" (free beach).

**Lidos (Private Beach Clubs):**

- **Lido di Bellagio:** This exclusive beach club offers a luxurious experience with a private beach, a swimming pool, a restaurant, and a bar. Day passes are available for purchase, providing access to all amenities.

- **Grand Hotel Tremezzo Beach:** This private beach, reserved for guests of the Grand Hotel Tremezzo, offers a glamorous setting with sun loungers, umbrellas, and attentive service.

- **Other Lidos:** Several other hotels and resorts around the lake offer private beach clubs for their guests.

**Secluded Swimming Areas:**

- **Coves and Bays:** Explore the lake's shoreline to discover hidden coves and bays, offering secluded swimming experiences away from the crowds.

- **Boat Access:** Rent a boat to access remote areas of the lake and find your own private swimming spot.

**Water Temperatures:**

- **Summer:** Lake Como's water temperature typically ranges from 20°C to 25°C (68°F to 77°F) in the summer months (June to August), making it pleasantly warm for swimming.
- **Spring and Autumn:** Water temperatures are cooler in the shoulder seasons, ranging from 15°C to 20°C (59°F to 68°F).

**Safety Considerations:**

- **Supervised Areas:** Swim in designated areas with lifeguard supervision whenever possible.
- **Water Depth:** Be aware of water depth, especially when swimming in unfamiliar areas.
- **Boat Traffic:** Pay attention to boat traffic, especially in areas with high boat activity.
- **Sun Protection:** Use sunscreen with a high SPF, wear a hat, and seek shade during the hottest part of the day.
- **Hydration:** Drink plenty of water to stay hydrated, especially in hot weather.

**Tips for Swimming Safety and Water Quality:**

- **Check for Warnings:** Pay attention to any posted warnings or flags indicating water conditions or hazards.

- **Avoid Swimming After Heavy Rain:** Heavy rain can affect water quality, so it's best to avoid swimming for a few days after a storm.

- **Be Aware of Currents:** Lake Como can have currents, especially near river mouths and narrow channels.

- **Swim with a Buddy:** Whenever possible, swim with a buddy for added safety.

- **Know Your Limits:** Don't overestimate your swimming abilities and stay within a safe distance from the shore.

By following these safety tips and choosing swimming spots wisely, you can enjoy a refreshing and safe swimming experience in the beautiful waters of Lake Como.

# CHAPTER 5: DINING

## Local Cuisine: Traditional Dishes to Try

Lake Como's culinary scene is a delightful fusion of fresh, local ingredients, traditional recipes, and regional influences. Prepare to tantalize your taste buds with delectable dishes that showcase the bounty of the lake and its surrounding mountains.

**From the Depths of the Lake:**

**Lake Fish:** The pristine waters of Lake Como yield a variety of freshwater fish that form the heart of many local specialties.

- **Perch (Pesce Persico):** Often served grilled or pan-fried, perch is prized for its delicate flavor and tender flesh. Try it in the classic dish, *risotto al pesce persico,* a creamy risotto infused with the essence of the lake.

- **Trout (Trota):** This flavorful fish is prepared in various ways, including grilled, baked, or smoked. Trout with polenta is a hearty and satisfying dish.

- **Whitefish (Lavarello):** Known for its delicate white flesh, whitefish is often served simply grilled or baked with herbs and lemon.

- **Missoltino (Missultin):** A unique local delicacy, missoltino is sun-dried shad (a type of herring) that is grilled or served with polenta. Its strong flavor is not for everyone, but it's a true taste of Lake Como tradition.

- **Alborelle:** These tiny fish are typically deep-fried and enjoyed as a crispy appetizer.

**Polenta: A Versatile Staple:**

Polenta, a creamy cornmeal dish, is a cornerstone of Northern Italian cuisine and features prominently in Lake Como's culinary traditions.

- **Polenta Uncia:** This classic dish features creamy polenta enriched with butter and local cheese, often served as a comforting side or a hearty main course.

- **Polenta Taragna:** A variation made with buckwheat flour, giving it a slightly nutty flavor. It's often served with melted cheese and butter.

- **Polenta con Funghi:** Polenta topped with sautéed wild mushrooms, a seasonal delicacy.
- **Polenta e Brasato:** Polenta served alongside braised beef, a rich and flavorful combination.

**Risotto: A Celebration of Rice:**

Risotto, a creamy rice dish, is another staple of Northern Italian cuisine, and Lake Como boasts its own regional variations.

- **Risotto al Pesce Persico:** As mentioned earlier, this classic dish combines creamy risotto with the delicate flavor of perch.
- **Risotto con Funghi Porcini:** Risotto infused with the earthy aroma of porcini mushrooms, a seasonal treat.
- **Risotto alla Milanese:** A saffron-infused risotto, often served with osso buco (braised veal shanks).

**Cheese: Local Treasures:**

The mountainous terrain surrounding Lake Como provides ideal pastures for grazing, resulting in a variety of delicious local cheeses.

- **Taleggio:** A soft, washed-rind cheese with a pungent aroma and creamy texture. Enjoy it on its own, melted on polenta, or in risotto.

- **Gorgonzola:** A blue cheese with a distinctive flavor and creamy texture. It's often used in salads, pasta dishes, or enjoyed with fruit and honey.

- **Formaggio d'Alpe:** A semi-hard cheese made from cow's milk, produced in the alpine pastures. It has a rich flavor and is often enjoyed with polenta or bread.

**Other Regional Specialties and Desserts:**

- **Bresaola:** Air-dried, salted beef, thinly sliced and served as an appetizer.

- **Sciatt:** Crispy buckwheat fritters filled with melted cheese, a popular snack in the Valtellina valley.

- **Miascia:** A sweet cake made with cornmeal, dried fruit, and nuts.

- **Panettone:** A traditional sweet bread enjoyed during the Christmas season.

**Food Markets and Local Producers:**

- **Como:** The city of Como hosts a weekly market on Tuesdays and Thursdays, where you can find fresh produce, cheese, cured meats, and other local specialties.

- **Menaggio:** Menaggio has a weekly market on Fridays, offering a variety of local products.

- **Varenna:** Varenna has a smaller market on Tuesdays, with a focus on fresh produce and local crafts.

- **Agriturismos:** Consider visiting agriturismos (farm stays) to experience farm-to-table dining and purchase locally produced cheese, honey, and other products.

# Top Restaurants

**Bellagio:**

**Fine Dining:**

- **Mistral (Grand Hotel Villa Serbelloni):** This Michelin-starred restaurant boasts innovative cuisine with a focus on seasonal ingredients and breathtaking lake views. (**Cuisine:** Modern Italian, **Atmosphere:** Elegant, **Reservations:** Essential, **Website:** https://www.villaserbelloni.com/it/mistral-restaurant.html)

- **La Terrazza (Hotel Splendide Royal):** Enjoy refined Italian cuisine with panoramic lake views from the elegant terrace. (**Cuisine:** Classic Italian with a modern twist, **Atmosphere:** Sophisticated, **Reservations:** Recommended, **Website:** https://www.splendideroyal.com/en)

**Traditional Trattorias:**

- **Trattoria San Giacomo:** This family-run trattoria serves authentic local dishes in a cozy and welcoming atmosphere. (**Cuisine:** Traditional Italian, **Atmosphere:** Rustic and charming, **Reservations:** Recommended, **Phone:** +39 031 950238)

- **La Grotta:** Tucked away in a charming alley, La Grotta offers a romantic setting and delicious homemade pasta dishes. (**Cuisine:** Italian, specializing in pasta,

**Atmosphere:** Intimate, **Reservations:** Recommended, **Phone:** +39 031 950353)

## Pizzerias:

- **La Lanterna:** This popular pizzeria serves wood-fired pizzas with fresh toppings in a casual setting. (**Cuisine:** Pizza, **Atmosphere:** Relaxed, **Reservations:** Not required, **Phone:** +39 031 951029)

## Cafes and Bars:

- **Bar Pasticceria Cavour:** Enjoy coffee, pastries, and light meals with lake views from this charming cafe. (**Cuisine:** Cafe, pastries, **Atmosphere:** Casual, **Reservations:** Not required)

- **Aperitivo at Hotel Belvedere:** Savor cocktails and appetizers with panoramic views from the terrace of Hotel Belvedere. (**Cuisine:** Bar snacks, **Atmosphere:** Stylish, **Reservations:** Recommended for terrace seating)

**Varenna:**

**Fine Dining:**

- **Royal Gourmet (Hotel Royal Victoria):** Experience fine dining with a focus on local ingredients and innovative techniques. (**Cuisine:** Modern Italian, **Atmosphere:** Elegant, **Reservations:** Essential, **Website:** https://www.rcollectionhotels.it/en/hotel-royal-victoria/catering-4-star-hotel-lake-como)

**Traditional Trattorias:**

- **Vecchia Varenna:** This charming trattoria offers classic Italian dishes and lake fish specialties in a rustic setting. (**Cuisine:** Traditional Italian, **Atmosphere:** Cozy, **Reservations:** Recommended, **Phone:** +39 0341 830361)

- **Il Cavatappi:** Enjoy homemade pasta and regional specialties in this intimate restaurant with a focus on local ingredients. (**Cuisine:** Italian, specializing in pasta, **Atmosphere:** Romantic, **Reservations:** Recommended, **Phone:** +39 0341 830283)

**Cafes and Bars:**

- **Caffè Varenna:** Relax with a coffee or aperitivo and enjoy lake views from this waterfront cafe. (**Cuisine:** Cafe, light meals, **Atmosphere:** Relaxed, **Reservations:** Not required)

**Menaggio:**

**Fine Dining:**

- **La Darsena (Grand Hotel Menaggio):** This elegant restaurant offers refined Italian cuisine with stunning lake views. (**Cuisine:** Modern Italian, **Atmosphere:** Sophisticated, **Reservations:** Recommended, **Website:** https://www.grandhotelmenaggio.com/)

**Traditional Trattorias:**

- **Osteria del Platano:** This family-run osteria serves hearty local dishes and pizzas in a warm and welcoming atmosphere. (**Cuisine:** Traditional Italian, pizza, **Atmosphere:** Casual, **Reservations:** Recommended, **Phone:** +39 0344 30257)

**Pizzerias:**

- **Pizzeria Lugano:** Enjoy classic wood-fired pizzas with a variety of toppings at this popular pizzeria. (**Cuisine:** Pizza, **Atmosphere:** Lively, **Reservations:** Not required, **Phone:** +39 0344 32005)

**Cafes and Bars:**

- **Caffè Centrale:** This central cafe is a great spot for people-watching and enjoying a coffee or gelato. (**Cuisine:** Cafe, gelato, **Atmosphere:** Lively, **Reservations:** Not required)

**Reservation Tips:**

- During peak season (June to August), reservations are highly recommended, especially for fine dining restaurants and popular trattorias.

- Many restaurants offer online reservation systems through their websites or platforms like TheFork.

- For smaller establishments, it's best to call ahead to secure a table.

- If you're unable to get a reservation, consider dining during off-peak hours or exploring restaurants in less touristy areas.

# CHAPTER 6: ACCOMMODATION

## Luxury Hotels

For those seeking an indulgent escape, Lake Como offers a collection of luxurious hotels that redefine lakeside splendor. Immerse yourself in opulent surroundings, breathtaking views, and impeccable service at these exceptional properties.

**Grand Hotel Tremezzo:**

This iconic hotel, a landmark on Lake Como since 1910, seamlessly blends Belle Époque grandeur with modern comforts.

- **Art Nouveau Style:** The hotel's façade is a masterpiece of Art Nouveau architecture, with ornate details and vibrant colors. Inside, you'll find elegant interiors, Murano glass chandeliers, and antique furnishings.

- **Opulent Amenities:** Enjoy three swimming pools (including a floating pool on the lake!), a private beach, a lavish spa, and multiple restaurants and bars.

- **Stunning Views:** Most rooms and suites offer breathtaking views of the lake and surrounding mountains.

- **Impeccable Service:** Experience personalized service and attention to detail that will make your stay truly unforgettable.

**Unique Features:**

- **T Beach:** A private beach with direct access to the lake, offering a glamorous setting for sunbathing and swimming.

- **Flowers Pool:** A stunning infinity pool surrounded by colorful flowers, offering panoramic lake views.

- **T Spa:** A luxurious spa with a range of treatments and therapies inspired by the lake's natural beauty.

- **Guest Experiences:** Guests rave about the hotel's elegant atmosphere, exceptional service, and prime location.

- **Contact Information:** Via Regina, 8, 22016 Tremezzina CO, **Website:** www.grandhoteltremezzo.com, **Phone:** +39 0344 42491

## Villa La Rosa B&B:

This elegant bed and breakfast, housed in a historic villa, offers a more intimate and personalized luxury experience.

- **Panoramic Views:** Perched on a hillside in Bellagio, Villa La Rosa offers stunning views of the lake and surrounding mountains.

- **Personalized Service:** The attentive hosts provide a warm welcome and personalized service, ensuring a memorable stay.

- **Elegant Interiors:** The villa features beautifully decorated rooms with antique furnishings, creating a refined and comfortable atmosphere.

Unique Features:

- **Beautiful Gardens:** Relax in the villa's lush gardens, featuring a variety of flowers, trees, and a panoramic terrace.

- **Gourmet Breakfast:** Start your day with a delicious breakfast featuring local specialties and homemade pastries.

- **Guest Experiences:** Guests appreciate the villa's tranquil setting, stunning views, and warm hospitality.
- **Contact Information:** Via Dei Pini, 26, 22021 Bellagio CO, **Phone:** +39 031 950320

**Other Luxury Hotels around the Lake:**

- **Mandarin Oriental, Lago di Como:** This stylish hotel offers contemporary design, a serene spa, and exceptional dining. (**Location:** Blevio)
- **Il Sereno Lago di Como:** This modern hotel boasts minimalist design, a waterfront setting, and a Michelin-starred restaurant. (**Location:** Torno, **Website:** www.ilsereno.com)
- **Villa d'Este:** This historic hotel, once a royal residence, offers timeless elegance, lush gardens, and a world-renowned spa. (**Location:** Cernobbio, **Website:** www.villadeste.com)

**Booking Tips:**

- **Book in Advance:** Luxury hotels on Lake Como are in high demand, especially during peak season. Book well in advance to secure your preferred dates and room type.
- **Consider Packages and Offers:** Many hotels offer special packages and deals, including spa treatments, dining credits, and activities.

- **Read Reviews:** Check online reviews from previous guests to get insights into the hotel's service, amenities, and overall experience.

- **Contact the Hotel Directly:** If you have specific requests or questions, contact the hotel directly to ensure your needs are met.

## Budget Options

Lake Como doesn't have to be an exclusively luxurious destination. With a bit of savvy planning, you can find comfortable and charming accommodations that won't break the bank.

Here's a selection of budget-friendly options in various towns and villages, offering excellent value for your money.

### Como Town:

- **Ostello Bello Lake Como:** This highly-rated hostel offers both private rooms and dorms in a social and vibrant atmosphere. Free breakfast and dinner are included, along with communal spaces, a bar, and organized events. (**Price range:** Dorms from €25, private rooms from €70, **Website:** https://ostellobello.com/en/hostel/como/)

- **B&B Vista Lago:** Enjoy stunning lake views from this cozy B&B, located a short walk from the historic center. Rooms are simply furnished but comfortable, and a delicious breakfast is included. (**Price range:** From €70)

- **Hotel Engadina:** This family-run hotel offers basic but clean and comfortable rooms within walking distance of Como's main attractions. (**Price range:** From €60)

### Bellagio:

- **Hotel Bellagio:** This centrally located hotel offers simple rooms with private bathrooms at affordable rates. Enjoy a continental breakfast and easy access to Bellagio's shops and restaurants. (**Price range:** From €80)

- **La Terrazza sul Lago:** This guesthouse offers rooms with balconies overlooking the lake, providing stunning views at a reasonable price. (**Price range:** From €90)

### Varenna:

- **Albergo Milano:** This family-run hotel offers cozy rooms with a traditional feel and a friendly atmosphere. It's located a short walk from the lakefront and Varenna's main attractions. (**Price range:** From €75)

- **Locanda Cavallino:** This charming guesthouse offers simple but comfortable rooms in a quiet location near the ferry terminal. (**Price range:** From €65)

**Menaggio:**

- **Hotel Menaggio:** This traditional hotel offers comfortable rooms and a central location, making it a convenient base for exploring Menaggio and the surrounding area. (**Price range:** From €70)

- **La Primula Hostel:** This hostel offers basic dorms and private rooms with shared bathrooms, a budget-friendly option for solo travelers and groups. (**Price range:** Dorms from €20, private rooms from €50, **Website:** http://www.lakecomohostel.com/)

**Booking Tips:**

- **Book in Advance:** Especially during peak season (June to August), booking your accommodation well in advance is essential to secure the best rates and availability.

- **Consider Location:** Think about your priorities. Do you want to be in the heart of a bustling town or in a quieter village? Factor in proximity to transportation and attractions.

- **Read Reviews:** Check online reviews from previous guests to get an idea of the accommodation's cleanliness, comfort, and overall value.

- **Look for Deals:** Many hotels and B&Bs offer special deals and discounts, especially during the shoulder seasons (spring and autumn) or for longer stays.

- **Compare Prices:** Use online booking platforms to compare prices and find the best deals for your chosen dates and location.

By considering these budget-friendly options and booking tips, you can enjoy a comfortable and enjoyable stay on Lake Como without overspending.

## Unique Stays

For a truly immersive and unforgettable experience on Lake Como, consider opting for a unique stay that goes beyond the traditional hotel experience. From luxurious villas with private pools to charming boutique hotels with distinct character, these options offer a personalized and intimate way to experience the lake's magic.

### Villa Rentals:

Imagine waking up to panoramic lake views from your private terrace, taking a dip in your own pool, and enjoying al fresco dining in a lush garden. Villa rentals offer the ultimate in privacy, space, and personalized service.

### Distinctive Features:

- **Privacy and Exclusivity:** Enjoy the freedom and seclusion of your own private villa, away from the crowds and bustle of hotels.

- **Spacious Accommodations:** Villas typically offer ample space for families or groups, with multiple bedrooms, living areas, and fully equipped kitchens.

- **Outdoor Living:** Many villas feature private gardens, terraces, and swimming pools, allowing you to fully embrace the beauty of Lake Como's surroundings.

- **Personalized Service:** Some villa rentals include concierge services, housekeeping, and even private chefs, catering to your every need.

Examples:

- **Villa La Cassinella:** This historic villa in Lenno boasts stunning lake views, a private pool, and lush gardens.

- **Villa del Sole:** This elegant villa in Tremezzo offers a private pool, a spa, and direct lake access.

- **Villa Balbiano:** This opulent villa in Ossuccio, featured in the film "House of Gucci," offers lavish interiors, extensive gardens, and a private dock.

## Booking Platforms:

- **The Luxury Travel Book:** https://theluxurytravelbook.com/

- **Lake Como Property:**

- **Airbnb Luxe:** https://www.airbnb.com/luxury

- **Onefinestay:** https://www.onefinestay.com/

**Boutique Hotels:**

Boutique hotels offer a more intimate and personalized experience compared to larger chain hotels. They often feature unique design elements, local charm, and attentive service.

**Distinctive Features:**

- **Unique Design and Character:** Boutique hotels often showcase distinctive architectural styles, interior design, and personalized touches that reflect the local culture and history.

- **Intimate Atmosphere:** With fewer rooms and a focus on personalized service, boutique hotels create a welcoming and cozy environment.

- **Local Experiences:** Many boutique hotels offer curated experiences, such as cooking classes, wine tastings, and guided tours, allowing you to immerse yourself in the local culture.

**Examples:**

- **Il Sereno Lago di Como:** This stylish hotel in Torno features contemporary design, a waterfront location, and a Michelin-starred restaurant. (**Website:** https://www.ilsereno.com/)

- **Villa d'Este:** This iconic hotel in Cernobbio exudes old-world glamour with its historic architecture, lush gardens, and impeccable service. (**Website:** https://www.villadeste.com/en)
- **Grand Hotel Tremezzo:** This Art Nouveau masterpiece in Tremezzo offers a blend of historic charm and modern luxury, with stunning lake views and a vibrant atmosphere. (**Website:** https://www.grandhoteltremezzo.com/)

**Booking Platforms:**

- **Mr & Mrs Smith:** https://www.mrandmrssmith.com/
- **Tablet Hotels:** https://www.tablethotels.com/
- **Design Hotels:** https://www.designhotels.com/

**Farm Stays and Agriturismos:**

For a truly authentic experience, consider a farm stay or agriturismo, where you can connect with nature, enjoy farm-fresh cuisine, and learn about local agricultural traditions.

**Distinctive Features:**

- **Rural Setting:** Escape the hustle and bustle and enjoy the tranquility of a countryside setting.

- **Farm-to-Table Cuisine:** Savor meals prepared with fresh, locally sourced ingredients, often grown on the property.

- **Authentic Experiences:** Participate in farm activities, such as harvesting fruits and vegetables, cheese-making, or wine tasting.

**Examples:**

- **Agriturismo Ferdy:** This family-run agriturismo in Bellagio offers charming rooms, organic produce, and stunning views.

- **Agriturismo Sorsasso:** This agriturismo in Domaso offers comfortable accommodations, a restaurant serving traditional dishes, and a vineyard producing local wines.

**Booking Platforms:**

- **Agriturismo.it:** https://www.agriturismo.it/

- **Farm Stay Planet:** https://www.farmstayplanet.com/

By choosing a unique stay on Lake Como, you'll create a truly personalized and memorable experience that goes beyond the ordinary.

# CHAPTER 7: BEST TIME TO VISIT

## Seasonal Highlights

Lake Como, with its diverse landscape and range of activities, offers unique charms in every season. Whether you dream of basking in the summer sun, hiking amidst autumnal hues, or enjoying the tranquility of a winter escape, understanding the nuances of each season will help you plan the perfect trip.

**Spring (March - May):**

- **Weather:** Mild temperatures (10-20°C / 50-68°F) with occasional rain showers. Days become progressively warmer and sunnier as spring progresses.

- **Crowds:** Fewer crowds compared to the peak summer months, offering a more relaxed atmosphere.

- **Highlights:**

- o **Blooming Flowers:** Witness the landscape come alive with vibrant colors as azaleas, rhododendrons, and wisteria burst into bloom.

- o **Pleasant Hiking:** Enjoy comfortable temperatures for hiking and exploring the surrounding hills and mountains.

- o **Villa Gardens:** Admire the manicured gardens of the villas in their springtime splendor.

- o **Easter Festivities:** Experience the cultural traditions of Easter celebrations in local towns and villages.

**Summer (June - August):**

- **Weather:** Warm and sunny with average temperatures around 25-30°C (77-86°F). July and August are typically the hottest months.

- **Crowds:** Peak season with increased crowds, especially in popular tourist areas.

- **Highlights:**

  - o **Water Activities:** Ideal conditions for swimming, boating, kayaking, and other water sports.

  - o **Outdoor Dining:** Enjoy al fresco dining with stunning lake views at restaurants and cafes.

- **Festivals and Events:** Experience lively summer festivals and events, including the Lake Como Film Festival.
- **Long Days:** Make the most of extended daylight hours for sightseeing and outdoor activities.

**Autumn (September - November):**

- **Weather:** Pleasant temperatures (15-20°C / 59-68°F) with crisp air and sunny days. Rainfall increases in November.
- **Crowds:** Fewer crowds compared to summer, offering a more tranquil atmosphere.
- **Highlights:**
  - **Fall Foliage:** Witness the stunning transformation of the landscape as leaves turn vibrant shades of red, orange, and yellow.
  - **Hiking and Biking:** Enjoy comfortable temperatures for exploring the trails and cycling routes.
  - **Harvest Season:** Savor seasonal delicacies like chestnuts, mushrooms, and local wines.
  - **Wine Festivals:** Participate in local wine festivals and enjoy tastings of regional wines.

**Winter (December - February):**

- **Weather:** Cool temperatures (5-10°C / 41-50°F) with occasional snowfall, especially in higher elevations.

- **Crowds:** The quietest season with minimal crowds, offering a peaceful escape.

- **Highlights:**
    - **Festive Atmosphere:** Experience the charm of Christmas markets and festive decorations in towns and villages.
    - **Winter Sports:** Enjoy skiing and snowboarding in the nearby mountains.
    - **Cozy Retreats:** Relax in cozy accommodations with fireplaces and enjoy the tranquility of the lake.
    - **Off-Season Deals:** Take advantage of lower prices on accommodations and travel.

**Considerations:**

- **Peak Season (June-August):** Expect higher prices and limited availability for accommodations and activities. Book well in advance.

- **Shoulder Seasons (April-May & September-October):** Offer a balance of pleasant weather, fewer crowds, and reasonable prices.

- **Off-Season (November-March):** Some attractions and restaurants may have limited hours or be closed. Ideal for those seeking tranquility and off-season deals.

## Events and Festivals

Lake Como's calendar is punctuated by vibrant events and festivals throughout the year, offering a glimpse into the region's rich cultural heritage and lively spirit. From film festivals to historic reenactments and festive Christmas markets, there's always something to celebrate on Lake Como.

**Spring:**

- **Concorso d'Eleganza Villa d'Este (May):** This prestigious event showcases vintage and classic cars in the elegant setting of Villa d'Este in Cernobbio. Admire these automotive masterpieces and enjoy the glamorous atmosphere. (**Location:** Cernobbio, **Website:** concorsodeleganzavilladeste.com)

- **Lake Como Comic Art Festival (May):** A relatively new festival celebrating comic art, with exhibitions, workshops, and meetings with renowned comic artists. (**Location:** Villa Erba, Cernobbio, **Website:** www.lccaf.com)

**Summer:**

- **Lake Como Film Festival (August/September):** This annual festival celebrates independent cinema, showcasing a diverse selection of films from around the world. Enjoy screenings, workshops, and discussions with filmmakers. (**Location:** Various venues around the lake, **Website:** www.lakecomofilmfestival.com)

- **Festival of San Giovanni (June 24th):** This traditional festival honors the patron saint of Como with a procession of boats on the lake, fireworks displays, and lively celebrations in Como town. (**Location:** Como)

- **Nameless Music Festival (May/June):** A major electronic music festival attracting international DJs and music lovers to the shores of Lake Como. (**Location:** Annone di Brianza, **Website:** www.namelessfestival.it)

- **LacMus Festival (July/August):** This international music festival features classical music concerts in stunning venues around the lake, including villas and historic churches. (**Location:** Tremezzina and other locations, **Website:** lacmusfestival.com)

**Autumn:**

- **Palio del Baradello (September):** This historic reenactment commemorates a medieval battle between Como and Milan. Witness costumed parades, archery competitions, and a lively atmosphere in the historic center of Como. (**Location:** Como)

- **Orticolario (October):** This unique event celebrates the art of gardening, with exhibitions, workshops, and a market showcasing rare plants, flowers, and garden design. (**Location:** Villa Erba, Cernobbio, **Website:** www.orticolario.it)

**Winter:**

- **Christmas Markets (December):** Embrace the festive spirit at charming Christmas markets in Como, Bellagio, and other towns around the lake. Browse stalls selling handcrafted gifts, decorations, and local delicacies, and enjoy the festive atmosphere. (**Location:** Various towns around the lake)

- **New Year's Eve Celebrations:** Many towns and villages host special events and fireworks displays to ring in the New Year.

**Other Local Events and Festivals:**

- **Festa di Sant'Abbondio (August 31st):** A religious festival in Como honoring the city's patron saint, with processions and celebrations.

- **Sagra dei Crotti (September):** A food festival celebrating the "crotti," natural caves used for storing food and wine. Enjoy local specialties and wine tastings in the Valchiavenna valley.

- **Autunno in Barco (October):** A series of events celebrating the autumn season in the Barco district of Como, with food stalls, music, and cultural activities.

**Tips for Attending Events and Festivals:**

- **Check dates and times:** Event dates and times can vary, so check official websites or local tourist information offices for the most up-to-date information.

- **Book accommodation in advance:** If you plan to attend a popular event, book your accommodation well in advance, as hotels and other lodgings tend to fill up quickly.

- **Purchase tickets early:** For events with ticketed entry, purchase tickets early to avoid disappointment.

- **Be prepared for crowds:** Popular events can attract large crowds, so be prepared for busy streets and venues.

- **Embrace the local culture:** Events and festivals are a great way to experience the local culture and traditions of Lake Como.

# CHAPTER 8: PRACTICAL INFORMATION

## Language: Basic Italian Phrases for Travelers

While English is spoken in many tourist areas around Lake Como, knowing a few basic Italian phrases can enhance your experience, demonstrate respect for the local culture, and open doors to more authentic interactions.

### Greetings and Introductions:

- **Buongiorno:** Good morning/good day (used until afternoon)
- **Buonasera:** Good evening/good afternoon (used from afternoon onwards)
- **Ciao:** Hello/goodbye (informal)

- **Grazie:** Thank you
- **Prego:** You're welcome/please
- **Mi scusi:** Excuse me
- **Sì:** Yes
- **No:** No
- **Non capisco:** I don't understand
- **Parla inglese?** Do you speak English?
- **Mi chiamo...:** My name is...
- **Piacere:** Nice to meet you

**Basic Phrases for Everyday Situations:**

- **Per favore:** Please
- **Scusi, dov'è...?** Excuse me, where is...?
- **Quanto costa?** How much does it cost?
- **Vorrei...:** I would like...
- **C'è un bancomat qui vicino?** Is there an ATM nearby?
- **A che ora apre/chiude?** What time does it open/close?
- **Ho bisogno di aiuto:** I need help

**Numbers and Currency:**

- **Uno, due, tre...:** One, two, three...
- **Dieci, venti, trenta...:** Ten, twenty, thirty...
- **Cento, duecento, trecento...:** One hundred, two hundred, three hundred...
- **Euro:** Euro (the currency of Italy)

**Ordering Food and Drinks:**

- **Un tavolo per due, per favore:** A table for two, please
- **Vorrei un menu, per favore:** I would like a menu, please
- **Cosa mi consiglia?** What do you recommend?
- **Vorrei ordinare...:** I would like to order...
- **Acqua naturale/frizzante:** Still/sparkling water
- **Un bicchiere di vino rosso/bianco:** A glass of red/white wine
- **Il conto, per favore:** The bill, please

**Asking for Directions and Transportation:**

- **Dov'è la stazione ferroviaria?** Where is the train station?
- **Dov'è la fermata dell'autobus?** Where is the bus stop?
- **Come posso arrivare a...?** How can I get to...?

- **Un biglietto per…, per favore:** A ticket to…, please
- **A destra/sinistra:** Right/left
- **Dritto:** Straight ahead

**Shopping and Bargaining:**

- **Quanto costa questo?** How much does this cost?
- **È troppo caro:** It's too expensive
- **Può farmi uno sconto?** Can you give me a discount?
- **Vorrei comprare questo:** I would like to buy this
- **Avete una taglia più grande/piccola?** Do you have a larger/smaller size?

**Additional Tips:**

- **Pronunciation:** Italian pronunciation is generally straightforward. Vowels are pronounced clearly, and most consonants sound similar to English.
- **Politeness:** Italians appreciate politeness. Use "per favore" (please) and "grazie" (thank you) frequently.
- **Body Language:** Italians often use hand gestures when speaking. Don't be afraid to use some gestures yourself to aid communication.

- **Patience:** Even if you struggle with the language, be patient and try your best. Most Italians will appreciate your effort.

- **Digital Tools:** Download a translation app on your phone for quick access to phrases and vocabulary.

## Currency

Italy, like most of the European Union, uses the **Euro (€)** as its official currency. Understanding the currency and payment methods will help you navigate your transactions smoothly during your Lake Como adventure.

**Euro (€):**

- **Banknotes:** Euro banknotes come in denominations of €5, €10, €20, €50, €100, €200, and €500. While the €200 and €500 notes are legal tender, they are less commonly used and some smaller businesses may not accept them.

- **Coins:** Euro coins are available in denominations of 1 cent, 2 cents, 5 cents, 10 cents, 20 cents, 50 cents, €1, and €2.

**Currency Exchange:**

- **Currency Exchange Bureaus:** You'll find currency exchange bureaus (cambio) at airports, train stations, and in tourist areas. Compare rates and fees before exchanging your money, as they can vary between providers.

- **Bank ATMs:** ATMs (bancomat) are widely available throughout Lake Como and offer a convenient way to withdraw Euros. Your bank may charge fees for international withdrawals, so check with your bank before your trip.

- **Credit Cards:** While credit cards are widely accepted in hotels, restaurants, and shops, it's always a good idea to carry some cash, especially for smaller purchases or in more rural areas.

**Credit Card Acceptance and Usage:**

- **Major Cards:** Visa and Mastercard are the most widely accepted credit cards in Italy. American Express is also accepted in many places, but less universally than Visa and Mastercard.

- **Chip and PIN:** Most credit card transactions in Italy require a chip and PIN. Make sure your card has a chip and that you know your PIN before your trip.

- **Contactless Payments:** Contactless payment methods, such as Apple Pay and Google Pay, are becoming increasingly popular in Italy.

**Tipping Customs and Expectations:**

- **Restaurants:** A service charge (coperto) is usually included in the bill, but it's customary to leave an additional tip of 5-10% for good service.

- **Bars and Cafes:** It's common to leave a small tip (around €1) for bar service.

- **Taxis:** Rounding up the fare to the nearest Euro or leaving a small tip (around 10%) is appreciated.

- **Hotels:** Tipping hotel staff, such as porters and housekeeping, is discretionary but appreciated.

**Practical Tips:**

- **Notify Your Bank:** Inform your bank of your travel dates to avoid any issues with using your cards abroad.

- **Check for Dynamic Currency Conversion:** When using your credit card, be aware of dynamic currency conversion (DCC). This allows you to pay in your home currency, but it often comes with unfavorable exchange rates. Choose to pay in Euros to get the best rate.

- **Keep Receipts:** Keep your receipts for all transactions, especially for larger purchases or currency exchanges.

# Safety Tips: General Safety Advice for Tourists

Lake Como is generally a safe destination for tourists, but it's always wise to be aware of your surroundings and take precautions to protect yourself and your belongings. Here are some general safety tips to ensure a worry-free trip.

**Pickpocketing and Theft Prevention:**

- **Be vigilant in crowded areas:** Pickpockets often target crowded areas like tourist attractions, markets, and public transportation. Be especially mindful of your belongings in these situations.

- **Secure your valuables:** Keep your valuables close to you at all times. Consider using a money belt or a secure bag that can be worn across your body.

- **Don't leave valuables unattended:** Never leave your bags, wallets, or phones unattended in public places, even for a short time.

- **Be wary of distractions:** Pickpockets often work in teams, using distractions to divert your attention while they steal your belongings.

- **Secure your accommodation:** Lock your hotel room door and windows when you leave, and use the safe provided for valuable items.

**Staying Safe on Public Transportation:**

- **Be aware of your surroundings:** Pay attention to your belongings and the people around you, especially during crowded times.

- **Keep your bags close:** Hold your bags close to you and avoid placing them on the floor or overhead racks where they are easily accessible.

- **Watch out for suspicious behavior:** If you see any suspicious behavior, report it to the driver or other passengers.

- **Validate your tickets:** Always validate your tickets before boarding public transportation to avoid fines.

**Avoiding Scams and Tourist Traps:**

- **Be wary of unsolicited offers:** Be cautious of people offering "free" gifts, bracelets, or other items, as they may demand payment after you accept.

- **Negotiate prices:** If you're unsure about a price, negotiate or ask for clarification before agreeing to a purchase.

- **Avoid unofficial taxis:** Use official taxis or pre-booked transportation services to avoid inflated fares or scams.

- **Research tours and activities:** Book tours and activities with reputable companies to avoid disappointment or scams.

- **Be cautious of "helpful" strangers:** Be wary of strangers who approach you offering help or directions, as they may be trying to scam you.

**Emergency Contact Numbers and Resources:**

- **General Emergency:** 112 (This number will connect you to police, ambulance, or fire services)

- **Police:** 113

- **Ambulance:** 118

- **Fire:** 115

- **Local Tourist Information Offices:** Tourist information offices can provide assistance with safety concerns, lost belongings, or other emergencies.

**Additional Safety Tips:**

- **Learn basic Italian phrases:** Knowing a few basic Italian phrases can be helpful in emergency situations.

- **Carry a copy of your passport:** Keep a copy of your passport and other important documents in a separate location from the originals.

- **Register with your embassy:** Consider registering your travel plans with your embassy or consulate in Italy.

- **Stay informed:** Stay updated on local news and any safety advisories issued by your government.

- **Trust your instincts:** If a situation feels unsafe or uncomfortable, remove yourself from it.

# CHAPTER 9: TRAVEL TIPS

## Transportation: Getting Around Lake Como

Navigating the picturesque towns and villages around Lake Como is an integral part of the experience. Whether you prefer the scenic routes of the ferries, the convenience of buses, or the personalized service of taxis and water taxis, understanding the transportation options will enhance your journey.

**Public Ferry Network and Routes:**

- **Navigazione Laghi:** The primary ferry operator on Lake Como, offering a comprehensive network of routes connecting major towns and villages.

- **Routes:** Ferries operate on various lines, traversing the lake's three branches and linking destinations like Como, Bellagio, Varenna, Menaggio, Tremezzo, and many more.

- **Types of Ferries:**

    o **Battello (Slow Ferry):** Traditional ferries offering a leisurely pace and scenic views.

    o **Aliscafo (Fast Ferry):** Hydrofoils providing faster connections between towns.

    o **Traghetto (Car Ferry):** Primarily for vehicle transport, but also carrying passengers, mainly between Varenna and Bellagio/Menaggio.

- **Timetables:** Timetables vary by season and route. Consult the Navigazione Laghi website (www.navigazionelaghi.it) or app for the most up-to-date schedules.

- **Tickets and Fares:** Purchase tickets at ferry terminals, on board (sometimes with a surcharge), or online. Fares are calculated based on distance and ferry type. Consider a day pass for unlimited travel if you plan to hop between villages.

**Bus Services and Schedules:**

- **ASF Autolinee:** The main bus operator in the Lake Como area, offering a network of routes connecting towns and villages not directly served by ferries.

- **Routes:** Buses cover a wide area, including routes along the lake shores and into the surrounding valleys.

- **Schedules:** Bus schedules vary by route and day of the week. Check the ASF Autolinee website (www.asfautolinee.it) or app for up-to-date information.
- **Tickets and Fares:** Purchase tickets from bus drivers, at ticket offices, or at designated kiosks. Fares are based on distance traveled.

## Taxi Services and Fares:

- **Availability:** Taxis are readily available in towns and villages around the lake, often stationed at taxi ranks near train stations, ferry terminals, and central squares.
- **Fares:** Taxi fares are metered, with an initial charge and a per-kilometer rate. Expect surcharges for nighttime rides, luggage, and travel on holidays.
- **Tips:** It's customary to round up the fare to the nearest Euro or leave a small tip (around 10%).

## Water Taxi Options and Costs:

- **Services:** Water taxis provide a personalized and convenient way to travel between specific points on the lake, offering flexibility and direct service.
- **Costs:** Fares are calculated based on distance, time, and the number of passengers. Expect to pay a premium for this exclusive service.

- **Booking:** Water taxis can be hailed at designated points or pre-booked through various companies.

## Tips for Navigating the Transportation System:

- **Plan your routes:** Use online resources like Google Maps or the Navigazione Laghi and ASF Autolinee websites to plan your journeys and check timetables.

- **Validate your tickets:** Always validate your bus and train tickets before boarding to avoid fines.

- **Be mindful of schedules:** Ferry and bus schedules can vary, especially on weekends and holidays. Allow extra time for your journeys.

- **Consider travel passes:** If you plan on using public transportation frequently, consider purchasing a travel pass for cost savings.

- **Combine transportation modes:** Combine ferries, buses, and taxis for optimal efficiency and to reach different areas of the lake.

- **Be aware of traffic:** Traffic can be heavy, especially during peak season and weekends. Allow extra time for your journeys by car or taxi.

- **Pack light:** If you're using public transportation, pack light to make your journeys more comfortable.

# Budgeting

Lake Como caters to a wide range of budgets, from backpackers seeking affordable adventures to luxury travelers indulging in the finer things. Here's a breakdown of estimated costs to help you plan your trip.

**Accommodation:**

- **Budget:**

    - Hostels: €20-€30 per night (dorm bed)

    - Budget hotels/guesthouses: €50-€80 per night (double room)

    - Camping: €15-€30 per night (per person)

- **Mid-Range:**

    - 3-star hotels: €80-€150 per night (double room)

    - B&Bs: €70-€120 per night (double room)

    - Apartments: €100-€200 per night

- **Luxury:**

    - 4- and 5-star hotels: €200-€500+ per night (double room)

    - Villas: €500-€2,000+ per night

**Food:**

- **Budget:**
  - Supermarket groceries: €50-€70 per week
  - Street food/casual meals: €10-€15 per meal
  - Pizzerias: €10-€15 per pizza
- **Mid-Range:**
  - Trattorias: €20-€30 per meal
  - Casual restaurants: €25-€40 per meal
- **Luxury:**
  - Fine dining restaurants: €50-€100+ per meal
  - Michelin-starred restaurants: €100-€200+ per meal

**Activities:**

- **Free Activities:**
  - Walking and hiking
  - Exploring towns and villages
  - Relaxing by the lake
  - Visiting churches and public gardens
- **Paid Activities:**

- Boat tours: €15-€50+ per person

- Villa visits: €8-€20+ per person

- Museums: €5-€15 per person

- Water sports: €20-€50+ per hour

- Cable car rides: €10-€20 per person

**Transportation:**

- **Public Transportation:**

  - Ferry tickets: €3-€15 per journey

  - Bus tickets: €2-€5 per journey

  - Train tickets: €5-€20+ per journey

- **Taxis:**

  - Starting fare: €5-€10

  - Per kilometer rate: €1-€2

- **Water taxis:**

  - €50-€100+ per journey

**Budgeting Tips:**

- **Travel during the shoulder seasons:** Accommodation and activities are generally cheaper in the spring (April-May) and autumn (September-October).

- **Consider self-catering:** Renting an apartment with a kitchen allows you to save money on meals by cooking some of your own food.

- **Take advantage of free activities:** Explore the many free attractions and activities Lake Como has to offer, such as hiking, walking tours, and visiting public gardens.

- **Use public transportation:** Public transportation is an affordable way to get around the lake. Consider purchasing a travel pass for multiple journeys.

- **Pack a reusable water bottle:** Tap water is safe to drink in Italy, so bring a reusable bottle to save money on bottled water.

- **Look for discounts and deals:** Check for discounts on attractions, tours, and activities online or at local tourist information offices.

- **Set a daily budget:** Determine a daily spending limit and track your expenses to stay within your budget.

By considering these estimated costs and budgeting tips, you can plan a Lake Como trip that aligns with your financial resources and travel style, ensuring a memorable and enjoyable experience without breaking the bank.

# Local Customs

Immersing yourself in the local culture is an enriching aspect of any travel experience. Understanding the customs and etiquette of Lake Como will not only enhance your interactions with locals but also demonstrate respect for their traditions and way of life.

**Dress Code for Different Occasions:**

- **General:** While Lake Como is a relatively relaxed destination, Italians generally take pride in their appearance. Opt for smart casual attire for everyday activities, such as exploring towns and villages, dining at casual restaurants, and visiting attractions.

- **Religious Sites:** When visiting churches and religious sites, dress modestly. Avoid wearing shorts, sleeveless tops, or revealing clothing. It's often customary to cover your shoulders and knees.

- **Fine Dining:** If you plan on dining at upscale restaurants, dress more formally. Men may consider wearing a jacket and tie, while women can opt for dresses or elegant separates.

- **Festivals and Events:** For local festivals and events, observe the dress code of the occasion. Some events may have specific attire requirements or traditional costumes.

### Dining Etiquette and Table Manners:

- **Greetings:** When entering a restaurant, greet the staff with "buongiorno" (good morning/day) or "buonasera" (good evening/afternoon).

- **Ordering:** Take your time to peruse the menu and ask for recommendations if needed. It's customary to order a starter (antipasto), a first course (primo piatto, usually pasta or risotto), a main course (secondo piatto, usually meat or fish), and possibly a dessert (dolce).

- **Bread:** Bread is usually served with meals. It's acceptable to tear off small pieces of bread and use them to mop up sauces.

- **Cutlery:** Use your fork and knife throughout the meal, even when eating pizza.

- **Pace Yourself:** Dining in Italy is often a leisurely affair. Take your time to savor each course and enjoy the conversation.

- **Paying the Bill:** The bill (il conto) is usually brought to the table. It's customary to leave a small tip (5-10%) for good service, even if a service charge (coperto) is included.

**Social Customs and Greetings:**

- **Greetings:** When meeting someone for the first time, a handshake is common. Among friends and family, cheek kisses (one on each cheek) are customary.

- **Personal Space:** Italians tend to stand closer together when conversing than people from some other cultures.

- **Eye Contact:** Maintaining eye contact during conversations is considered polite and shows respect.

- **Conversation:** Italians are generally expressive and animated when conversing. Don't be surprised by passionate discussions or hand gestures.

- **Respect for Elders:** Show respect for elders by using formal greetings ("Buongiorno" or "Buonasera") and offering them your seat on public transportation.

**Respecting Local Culture and Traditions:**

- **Learn basic Italian phrases:** Even a few basic phrases in Italian will be appreciated and show your willingness to engage with the local culture.

- **Respect religious customs:** Be mindful of religious customs and traditions, especially when visiting churches or during religious festivals.

- **Observe local etiquette:** Pay attention to local customs and etiquette in different situations, such as queuing, using public transportation, and interacting with shopkeepers.

- **Be mindful of noise levels:** Avoid being excessively loud or disruptive in public places, especially in residential areas or near historic sites.

- **Respect the environment:** Dispose of trash responsibly and avoid littering. Respect the natural beauty of Lake Como by staying on designated trails and avoiding disturbing wildlife.

# BONUS

## Map Guides

**BELLAGIO: THE PEARL OF LAKE COMO**

GET THERE WITH A QUICK SCAN! USE THIS QR CODE FOR EASY NAVIGATION.

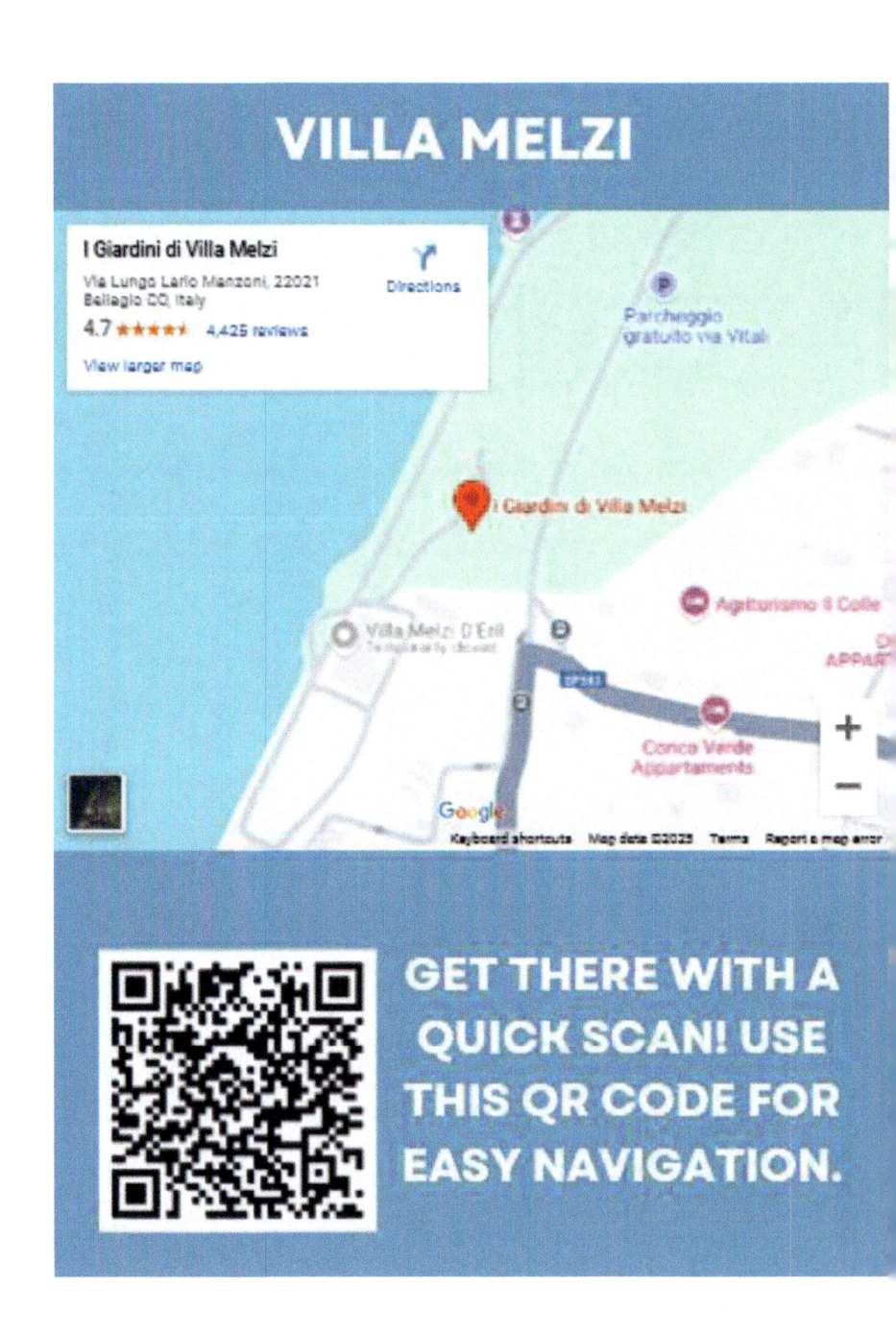

# VILLA MELZI

**I Giardini di Villa Melzi**
Via Lungo Lario Manzoni, 22021
Bellagio CO, Italy

**4.7** ★★★★★ 4,425 reviews

View larger map

**GET THERE WITH A QUICK SCAN! USE THIS QR CODE FOR EASY NAVIGATION.**

# VILLA DEL BALBIANELLO.

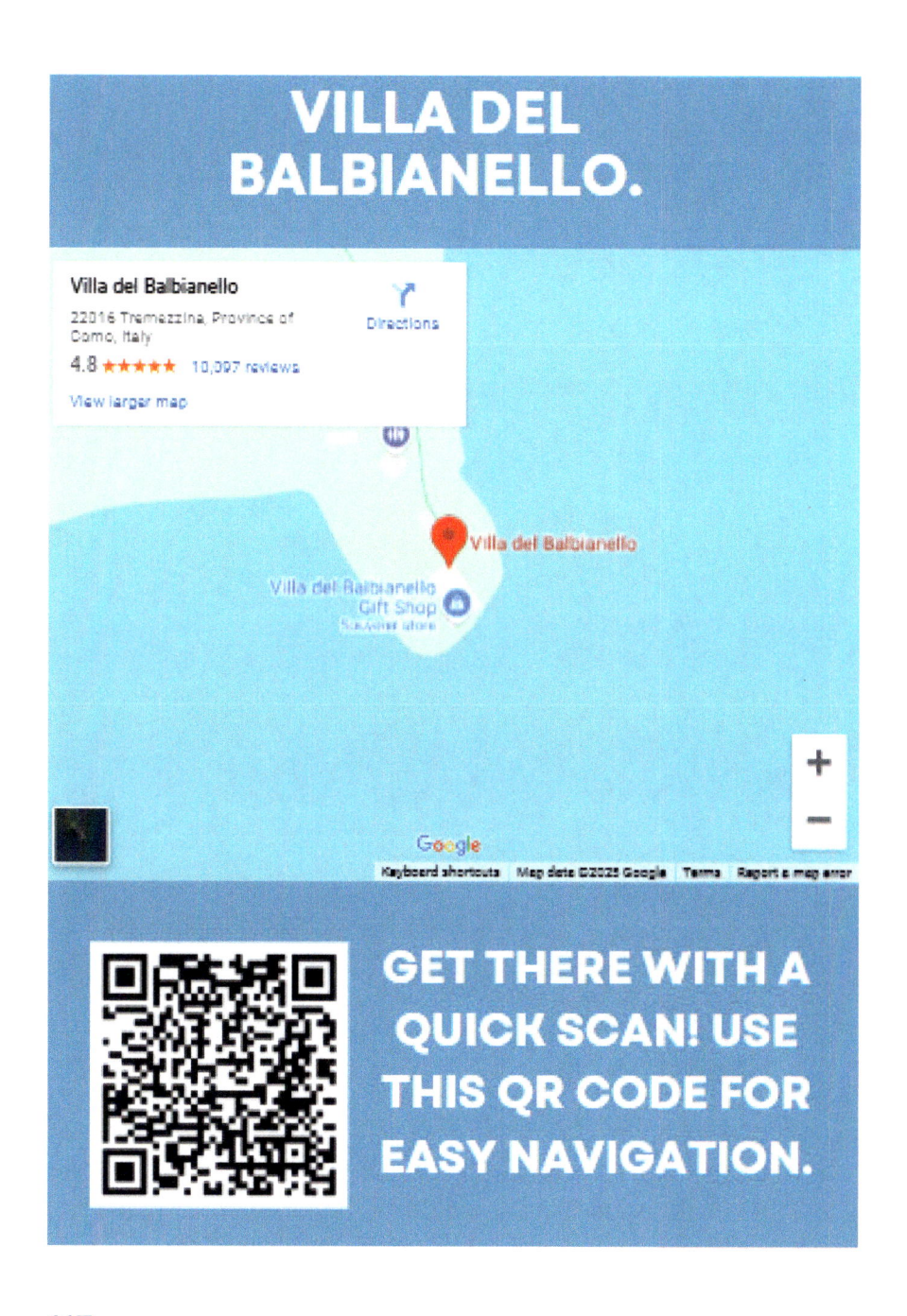

**Villa del Balbianello**
22016 Tremezzina, Province of Como, Italy
4.8 ★★★★★ 10,397 reviews
View larger map

**GET THERE WITH A QUICK SCAN! USE THIS QR CODE FOR EASY NAVIGATION.**

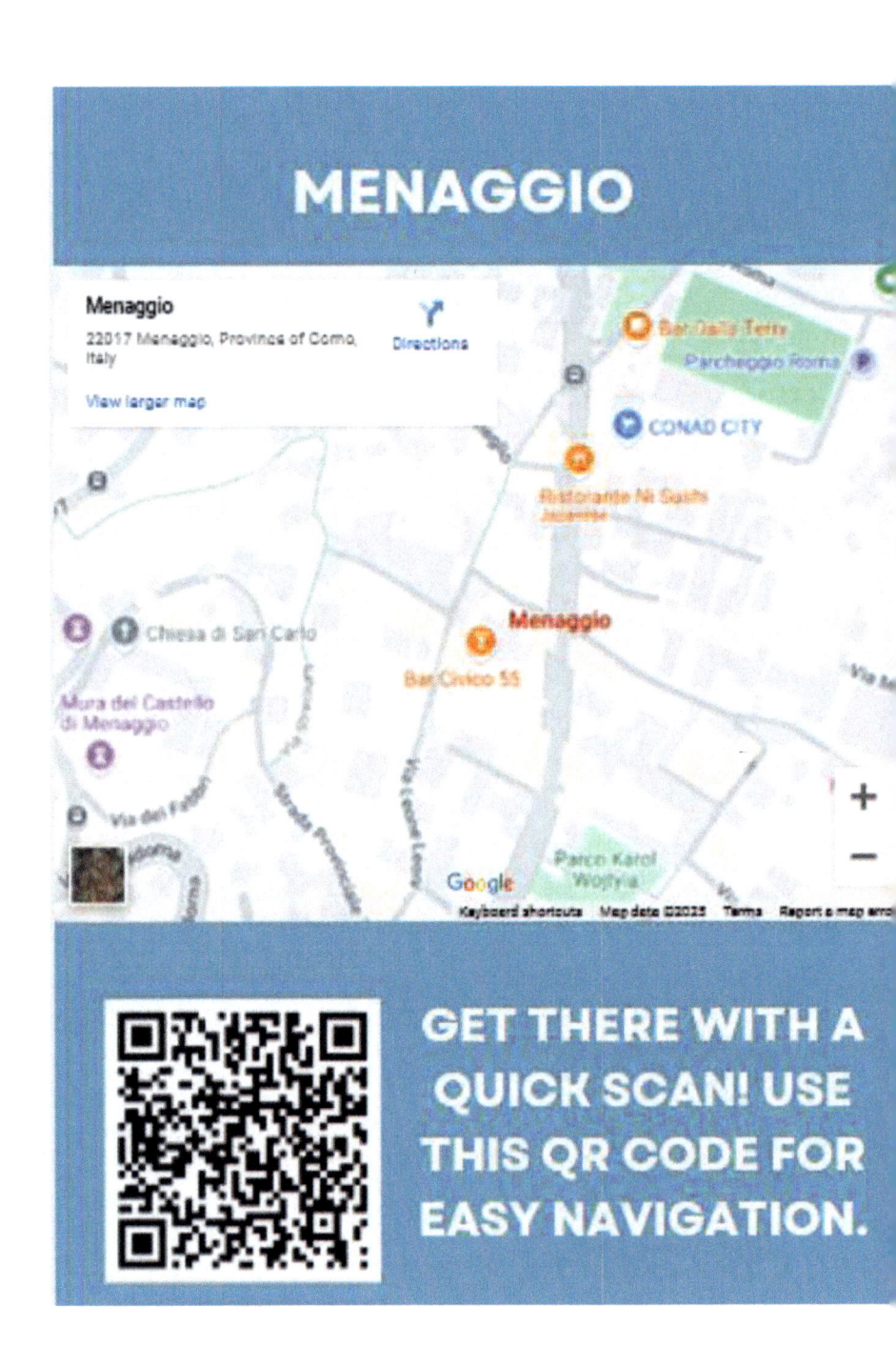

# MENAGGIO

**Menaggio**
22017 Menaggio, Province of Como, Italy

View larger map

**GET THERE WITH A QUICK SCAN! USE THIS QR CODE FOR EASY NAVIGATION.**

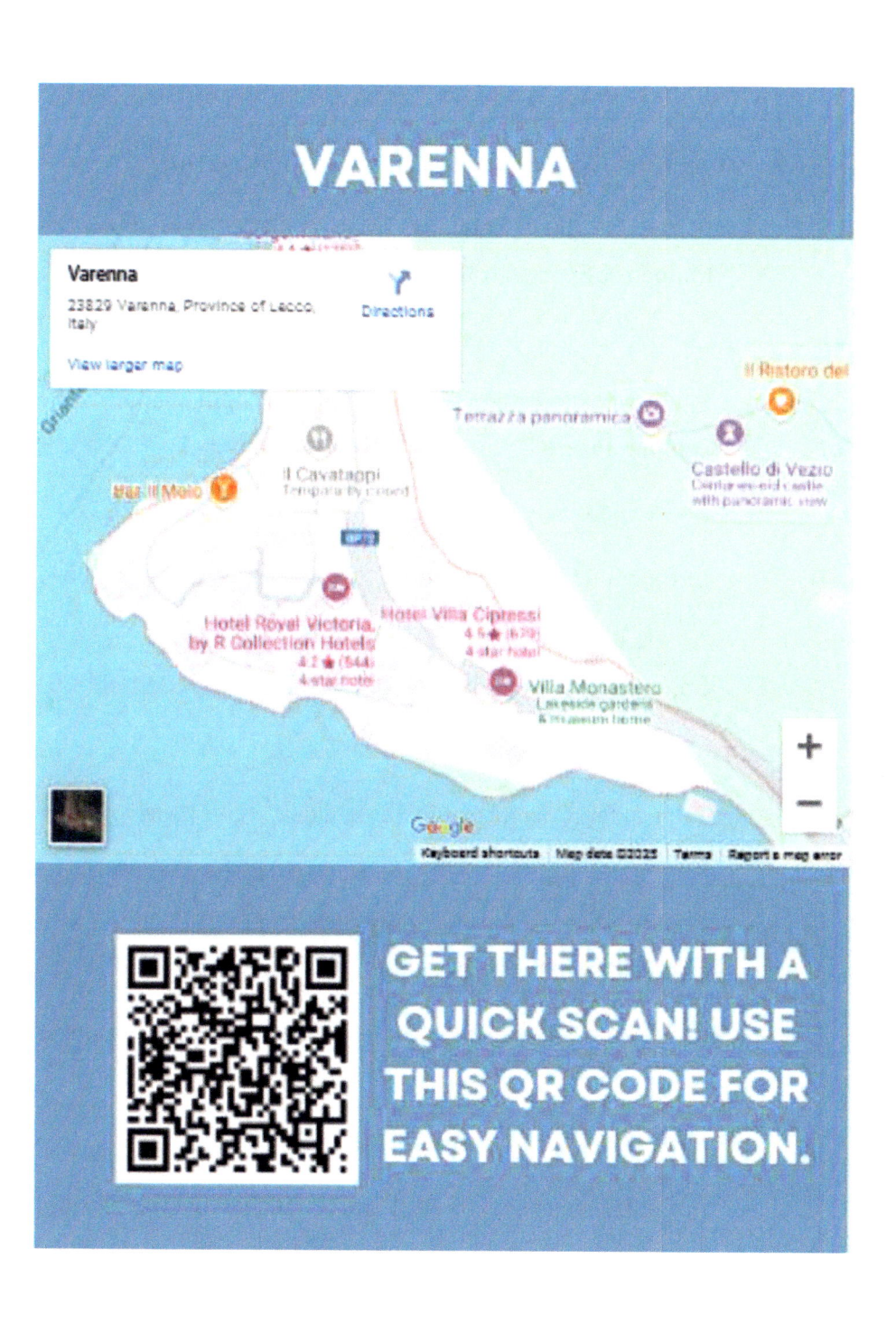

# VARENNA

**GET THERE WITH A QUICK SCAN! USE THIS QR CODE FOR EASY NAVIGATION.**

# One Week Itinerary

## Day 1: Arrival in Como and Lakeside Exploration

- Arrive at Milan Malpensa Airport (MXP) and take the Malpensa Express train to Como San Giovanni station.
- Check in to your hotel in Como.
- Explore the charming historic center of Como, including the Duomo, Piazza Cavour, and the Volta Temple.
- Enjoy a leisurely stroll along the lakefront promenade.
- In the afternoon, take a boat trip to the picturesque village of Cernobbio.
- Enjoy dinner with lake views at a restaurant in Cernobbio.

## Day 2: Bellagio - The Pearl of Lake Como

- Take a ferry from Como to Bellagio, the "Pearl of Lake Como."
- Wander through the charming streets of Bellagio, lined with colorful houses and shops.
- Visit Villa Melzi and its stunning gardens, enjoying panoramic lake views.
- Have lunch at a lakeside restaurant in Bellagio.
- In the afternoon, take a boat trip to Villa del Balbianello and explore its historic villa and terraced gardens.

- Enjoy a romantic dinner in Bellagio with breathtaking views.

## Day 3: Varenna and Hiking Adventures

- Take a ferry from Bellagio to Varenna, known for its colorful houses and relaxed atmosphere.

- Visit Villa Monastero and its beautiful botanical gardens.

- Hike the Sentiero del Viandante, a historic trail offering stunning lake views.

- Have lunch at a traditional trattoria in Varenna.

- In the afternoon, visit Castello di Vezio, a medieval castle perched on a hill overlooking the lake.

- Enjoy dinner with panoramic views at a restaurant in Varenna.

## Day 4: Menaggio and Lakeside Relaxation

- Take a ferry from Varenna to Menaggio, a lively resort town with a family-friendly atmosphere.

- Stroll along the lakefront promenade and enjoy the vibrant atmosphere.

- Relax at Lido di Menaggio, a public beach with swimming and sunbathing facilities.

- Have lunch at a lakeside cafe or restaurant.

- In the afternoon, rent a boat and explore the lake at your own pace.

- Enjoy a delicious dinner at a restaurant in Menaggio.

## Day 5: Villa Carlotta and Tremezzo

- Take a ferry from Menaggio to Tremezzo and visit Villa Carlotta, renowned for its art collection and botanical gardens.

- Explore the charming village of Tremezzo, known for its Grand Hotel Tremezzo and picturesque setting.

- Have lunch at a restaurant with lake views in Tremezzo.

- In the afternoon, take a leisurely walk along the Greenway del Lago di Como, enjoying the scenic lakeside path.

- Enjoy a farewell dinner at a restaurant in Tremezzo or Como.

## Day 6: Day Trip to Lugano or Milan

- Choose a day trip based on your interests:
    - **Lugano:** Take a boat trip across the lake to Lugano, Switzerland, and explore this charming city with its Italian-Swiss flair.
    - **Milan:** Take a train to Milan and experience the fashion, art, and culture of this vibrant city.

- Enjoy dinner in Lugano or Milan before returning to Lake Como.

**Day 7: Departure**

- Enjoy a final breakfast with lake views.

- Depart from Lake Como and travel to Milan Malpensa Airport (MXP) for your onward journey.

# CONCLUSION

As you close this guide, the images of Lake Como likely dance in your mind: the shimmering expanse of water reflecting the sky, the charming villages nestled amidst verdant hills, the elegant villas whispering tales of a bygone era.

Lake Como is a destination that captivates the senses and nourishes the soul. Whether you've been drawn to its shores by the promise of adventure, the allure of history, or the simple desire for tranquility, you're sure to find something truly special here.

This guide has offered a glimpse into the diverse experiences that await you. From exploring picturesque villages and historic villas to indulging in delectable cuisine and embarking on outdoor adventures, Lake Como offers something for everyone.

Now, it's your turn to write your own Lake Como story. Step onto the ferry, wander through the cobblestone streets, hike to breathtaking viewpoints, and savor the flavors of the region. Embrace the beauty, the culture, and the warmth of the Italian spirit.

As you embark on your journey, remember that the true magic of Lake Como lies in the moments you create. So, explore with an open heart, embrace the unexpected, and let the lake's enchantment weave its spell on you.

I hope this guide has inspired you to discover the wonders of Lake Como and that it serves as a valuable companion on your travels. I would be delighted to hear about your experiences and welcome your honest reviews and positive feedback. Your insights will help me refine this guide and ensure that it continues to inspire others to explore this captivating destination.

Printed in Great Britain
by Amazon